Closer to The Real Christmas Story
Insights into the biblical text, history, culture, and geography

Closer to The Real Christmas Story

Insights into the biblical text, history, culture, and geography

Jared Burkholder

Illustrations by Heather Marx

DORRANCE PUBLISHING CO., INC.
PITTSBURGH, PENNSYLVANIA 15222

All Rights Reserved
Copyright © 2012 by Jared Burkholder

No part of this book may be reproduced or transmitted, downloaded, distributed, reverse engineered, or stored in or introduced into any information storage and retrieval system, in any form or by any means, including photocopying and recording, whether electronic or mechanical, now known or hereinafter invented without permission in writing from the publisher.

Dorrance Publishing Co., Inc.
701 Smithfield Street
Pittsburgh, PA 15222
Visit our website at *www.dorrancebookstore.com*

ISBN: 978-1-4349-1199-5
eISBN: 978-1-4349-3908-1

This book is dedicated to our children, Brad, Tiffany, Jonathan and Candice whose inquisitive K-through-College minds challenged me every Christmas to separate Christmas fact from fiction in light of the biblical text and the historical context.

Acknowledgements

Many individuals have inspired me in the study of God's Word. Two in particular, however, stand out. The first is one of my seminary professors at Grace Theological Seminary, the late Dr. Charles Smith. Dr. Smith modeled a fresh, liberating, deep-seated commitment to what the biblical text actually says. He let his study of the biblical text drive his theology rather than superimposing his theology upon the text.

The second individual who particularly inspired me in the study of God's Word was Dr. Jim Monson, professor of historical geography at Jerusalem University College in Israel. My wife, Charlene, and I had the privilege of studying under Dr. Monson in January 1974. Jim's enthusiasm for the geographical, historical and cultural context of the biblical story and commitment to the details of the biblical text have inspired and guided my study and teaching of God's Word over these past decades.

I am also deeply indebted to the insights and persistence of Dr. Kenneth Bailey whose writings about the *manger* and the *inn* helped me finally make sense of the Christmas story and launched me on this literary voyage. And finally, I want to thank Dr. Rami Arav for his invaluable archaeological insights. Rami is a close personal friend, professor at the University of Nebraska at Omaha (Nebraska), and Director of the Bethsaida Excavations Project on the north shore of the Sea of Galilee. He and his wife, Naomi, grew up in northern Israel not far from Nazareth.

TABLE OF CONTENTS

Chapter		The Gifts of Christmas	Page
	Acknowledgements		vi
	Introduction		x
1	Single and Pregnant	(The Gift of Submission)	2
2	Hangin' with Relatives	(The Gift of Encouragement)	6
3	"Joseph, You May Take One Giant-Step"	(The Gift of a Healed Heart)	9
4	"It's Best We Get out of Town"	(The Gift of Protection)	13
5	"Where in the World is Beth-lehem?"	(The Gift of Safe Travel)	17
6	"Nuestra Casa Es Su Casa" ("Our House Is Your House")	(The Gift of Family)	21
7	Special Delivery	(The Gifts of Life and Individuality)	25
8	The Scavenger Hunt	(The Gift of Special Revelation)	28

Chapter	The Gifts of Christmas		Page
9	The Original Hallelujah Chorus	(The Gift of Praise)	31
10	Law-Abiding Citizens	(The Gift of Stewardship)	34
11	Two Prophets and a Baby	(The Gift of Affirmation)	37
12	For God So Loved the "Wise Guys"	(The Gift of Cultural Diversity)	41
13	Star Trek	(The Gift of Divine Guidance)	44
14	Pay It Forward	(The Gift of Timely Provision)	48
15	Murder, He Wrote	(The Gift of Salvation)	52
16	"Are We There Yet?"	(The Gift of God's Faithfulness)	55
	Creator Christ, How Great Thou Art		59
	Endnotes: Insights into the biblical text, culture, history and geography		61
	Works Cited		108

CHANCE Encounter at the END OF THE EARTH

I am in Mali, West Africa, for what I know could well be my last time. I have been in Mali many times before with students from Grace University and have always wanted to visit historically significant Timbuktu. I inquire about hitching a ride on a Mission Aviation Fellowship (MAF) charter flight to Timbuktu. A long story short: the flight has room for me; three gals visiting Mali are also on the flight; a sand storm scraps our planned landing and visit to Timbuktu; we are re-routed to the sub-Sahara city of Gao to take on fuel; we eat our sack lunches out on the tarmac in the 120-degree shade under one of the wings of our airplane.

On the return flight from Gao to Bamako, I *just so happen* to sit next to Heather, one of the gals visiting Mali and fiancé of Brian Marx, the MAF co-pilot. Soon after take-off, Heather takes out a sketch pad and pencil and continues drawing a nomadic tribeswoman sitting outside her *mobile home*. I am amazed. Heather is VERY good! A few questions later I find out Heather is from Baton Rouge, Louisiana. She is a professional artist, as is her mother. Heather's specialty is watercolors.

And so it is that high above the sand-reddened dust clouds of the Sahara Desert, on a flight to the *end of the earth* (as *Timbuktu* has come to symbolize in English culture and speech), Heather's and my paths providentially cross. Our Timbuktu disappointment is God's timely appointment! I tell Heather about this book I am writing and ask her if she would be interested in painting the illustrations. Heather accepts my invitation and the rest, as they say, is history ... in this case quite literally, "His-story!" Brian and Heather are married and presently serving with Mission Aviation Fellowship in Indonesia.

INTRODUCTION

Christmas is without question the most festive event on the Christian calendar, and the birth of Jesus is arguably one of the most popular Bible stories. Every December, around the world, millions of Christmas messages are preached, Sunday school programs presented, carols sung, Sunday school lessons taught, videos and DVD's watched, and Christmas story books read. There is nothing quite like a spiritual, planet-rescuing mission involving ancient prophecies, angelic messengers, supernatural dreams, mysterious pregnancies, suspected sexual misconduct, political intrigue, foreign agents, common peasants, a royal birth, the slaughter of infants and an extra-terrestrial liberator to spark our interest, stir our emotions and fuel our imaginations.

However, while the central theological message of Christmas is clear (that Jesus is God in human flesh, thereby able to rescue humanity from the power and penalty for sin), and that while the great faith-developing message of Christmas is clear (that God is faithful and can be trusted no matter what the circumstances), not so clear for us who read these accounts 2000 years later is how all the details of the Nativity harmoniously and chronologically fit together. Matthew and Luke's very different perspectives on Jesus' birth bristle with questions itching to be answered.

How far along, for example, is Mary in her pregnancy when she and Joseph leave for Bethlehem? From a human perspective, why do Joseph and Mary not wait until after Jesus is born before traveling to Bethlehem? Does it make sense that Mary's family would send Mary off to Bethlehem so close to Mary giving birth to her first child (as assumed by the traditional Christmas story) if they have no idea where they are going to stay? Is Mary and Joseph's only plan to stay in Bethlehem's inn and deliver Mary's first baby themselves? Are there really no relatives in Bethlehem, Joseph's ancestral home town, with whom Joseph and Mary can stay? How far from Bethlehem do Elizabeth and Zacharias live? How much do we know about Caesar Augustus' decree? Does the decree create a sense of urgency by setting a deadline? Were Joseph and Mary all by themselves in the stable? When did the star appear in relation to Jesus' birth? Did the wise men follow the star to Jerusalem? In whose house are Joseph and Mary when the wise men arrive? Does it not seem strange that Joseph and Mary supposedly have money to stay at the local *Motel 6,* but apparently not enough to buy a sacrificial lamb at the Temple?

Searching for answers and solutions to some of the above and other questions throughout virtually all my adult life, the journey got long. I was perplexed by issues that appeared illogical and frustrated by details that appeared contradictory. Until, that is, on an ordinary, vanilla afternoon, things changed!

It is December 2003 when suddenly, out of the blue, God surprises me! I am in the Grewcock Library on the campus of Grace University looking for a periodical. Not even thinking about Christmas at the moment my eyes fall on the *Christian Leader*, a Mennonite Brethren publication, sitting on a table. Having pastored a Mennonite Brethren church for nine years, I pick up the magazine, look over the Table of Contents and spot an article by Kenneth E. Bailey titled, *"The Manger and the Inn."* The article is an exposition of Luke 2:7, focusing on the meanings and usages of the two prominent nouns in that verse, "manger" and "inn." Bailey concludes that Joseph and Mary's experience in Bethlehem is significantly different than what is traditionally portrayed. I leave the library filled with excitement. Bailey has me "thinking outside the barn." In the weeks that follow, I am amazed at how Bailey's paradigm brings harmony and sensibility to the Christmas story taking shape in my mind, the ultimate result of which is this book.

I have not written this book therefore to be creative, controversial, or 100% correct and I make no claim that the version of the Christmas story presented in this book is exactly the way it happened 2000 years ago. What I do believe is that the textual and contextual evidence presented in the endnotes suggests this version of the Christmas story is much closer to historical fact and cultural reality than is the traditional version uncritically parroted every year with little or no thought given to the story as a whole.

Rather, I have written this book because I believe that getting the Christmas story right, matters! After all, it is God's Word which deserves our best attention and treatment. I am convinced that too many of us for too long have been too quick to give the traditional Christmas story a pass even when the pieces of the traditional Christmas story puzzle do not fit. My goal is not to win an argument but to engage in a discussion . . . to challenge the Church as a hermeneutical community of believers to take a new look at the Christmas story and the questions that swirl around the birth of Jesus. To that end I trust that my research, reasoning and conclusions will make a positive contribution to the interpretation and application of Matthew 1-2 and Luke 1-2. In particular, I pray that this book will help parents meaningfully discuss the Christmas story with their children of all ages and develop in them critical thinking skills. To accomplish this, I have divided this book into two main sections.

The first half of the book is the story itself. Consisting of 16 easy-to-read, bite-sized chapters, each beautifully illustrated by professional artist Heather Marx, the narrative provides for the reader insight into Jesus' birth *geographically, politically, chronologically, culturally, textually and logically*. It takes a little over 40 minutes to read the story out loud. The last half of the book consists of endnotes and commentary. The endnotes *factually* document, *biblically* cross-reference and/or *logically* discuss specific aspects of the story. The endnotes are keyed by page number back to the narrative for easy access.

Re-evaluating the Christmas story, however, is more than some kind of *biology lab experiment* to be dissected and analyzed intellectually like a "pickled" frog. Bible study is about life change. To that end each chapter concludes by highlighting one of the *Gifts of Christmas* embedded in that part of the story. All of the gifts call for a response, challenging us to integrate faith and life. "*For* (to paraphrase 1 Corinthians 13) *if I have all knowledge, and understand the Christmas story better now than I ever have before, but do not demonstrate God's sacrificial, gave-His-only-begotten-Son kind of love, then I am no more than a beautifully wrapped Christmas present with nothing inside."* ~ Jared Burkholder, 2012

Closer to The Real Christmas Story

Chapter 1
SINGLE AND PREGNANT
(Luke 1:26-38)

"... you will conceive in your womb, and bear a son ..." (Luke 1:31).

High above the Jezreel Valley, Mary pauses to drink in the spectacular view. On the eastern horizon, the sun hangs like a pomegranate in the morning haze, and before her, the broad, fertile valley welcomes a new day. From this high bluff, the road out of Nazareth snakes its way down the southern slope of the hills of Lower Galilee to the valley below.[1]

As a child, Mary and her friends often visited this scenic spot just outside of Nazareth where they playfully imagined what life was like in the valley and beyond. Those childhood experiences are now a distant memory. Mary stands beside Joseph, her husband, as a mature young woman in her late teens,[2] some five months pregnant.[3] The dramatic events of the past year are racing through Mary's head.

Mary's dream of someday getting married had been realized. The bridewealth had been negotiated by her family.[4] Family commitments had been made and legal formalities followed. Although the betrothal made her a legally married woman, Mary had looked forward to the day when she and Joseph would publicly enter the second stage of marriage and live together.[5]

Mary and Joseph's ordinary lives, however, were changed forever the day the angel Gabriel unexpectedly appeared to Mary.[6] After assuring Mary that God had chosen her for a special purpose, Gabriel told her that

Departure from Nazareth

she would conceive a baby boy. Her child would be called Son of the Most High! He would sit on David's throne and reign over the nation of Israel forever. His kingdom would have no end.[7]

Mary was thrilled that Israel's long-awaited Messiah was finally coming and was amazed that God had selected her to be His mother. Mary was confused, however, by Gabriel's statement that she was going to get pregnant. Mary was a virgin, committed to sexual purity.[8] She and Joseph were betrothed but not yet living together, and they had no plans to enter that second stage of marriage any time soon. In Mary's mind, her becoming pregnant was impossible. Mary asked Gabriel how it could be that she was going to get pregnant. Gabriel reminded Mary that nothing is impossible with God. He then explained that she would conceive a son when the Holy Spirit came upon her and the power of the Most High overshadowed her. God would be the child's father[9] and Mary the baby's virgin mother as prophesied by Isaiah.[10] Humbled, Mary willingly submitted to God's plans for her life.

Looking out across the beautiful Jezreel Valley, Mary's response to Gabriel still echoes in her ears, *"I am the Lord's slave. Be it done to me according to Your word."*[11]

The Gift of Submission

What persons, goals or ambitions could keep you from totally submitting to God's plans for your life the way Mary totally submitted to God's plans for her life?

Give This Gift to God Wholeheartedly!

"I urge you ... to present your bodies a living and holy sacrifice ... . And do not be conformed to this world, but be transformed by the renewing of your mind, that you may prove what the will of God is, that which is good and acceptable and perfect" (Romans 12:1-2).

Chapter 2

HANGIN' WITH RELATIVES

(Luke 1:5-25, 39-55)

"Mary arose and went with haste to the hill country ... of Judah" (Luke 1:39).

As Mary begins her second trip to Judea in the past six months, she vividly recalls the day she got pregnant. The Holy Spirit came upon her and the power of the Most High overshadowed her just like the angel Gabriel had said.[12] Mary, however, did not tell anyone that she was expecting a baby, not even Joseph or her parents.[13] What Mary did tell her family was that the angel Gabriel had visited her and had told her that their elderly relatives, Elizabeth and Zacharias, were pregnant. Elizabeth had kept this secret from even her closest friends for the past five months.[14] Mary remembers how excited her family had been when they heard the news.[15] Preparations had been made for her and several others[16] to travel to Judea immediately[17] to celebrate this special event.[18]

After nearly a week traveling, the women had arrived at the home of Zacharias and Elizabeth.[19] When Mary entered the house and greeted Elizabeth, however, Elizabeth's baby leaped in her womb. Startled by her baby's reaction and filled with the Holy Spirit, Elizabeth had cried out with a loud voice, "Blessed among women are you, Mary, and blessed is the fruit of your womb! How is it that the mother of my Lord should come to me? For behold, when the sound of your greeting reached my ears, the baby leaped in my womb for joy."[20] Inspired by Elizabeth's blessing, Mary had raised her hands toward heaven and exalted the Lord.[21]

Farewell to Elizabeth

Unfortunately, Zacharias, Elizabeth's husband, could only look on silently. Months before, Zacharias had been carrying out his priestly duties in the Temple when the angel Gabriel had appeared to him and said, "Your request has been heard, Zacharias.[22] Your wife Elizabeth will bear you a son and you will name him John." Knowing, however, that he and Elizabeth were beyond the normal childbearing age, Zacharias had not believed Gabriel. God, therefore, punished Zacharias by taking away both his ability to hear[23] and speak until after the baby was born.[24]

For almost three months Mary had stayed with Elizabeth,[25] helping out wherever she could. Mary's extended visit provided Elizabeth with a friend to talk to and also gave Elizabeth and other elderly relatives the opportunity to prepare Mary for marriage, childbirth and mothering.[26] Righteous Elizabeth,[27] who had patiently waited for God to answer her prayers, repeatedly encouraged Mary to always trust God no matter how difficult the circumstances and to always obey God no matter what the cost.

The day finally came, however, for Mary to return home. Sad to leave but anxious to get back home, Mary had given Elizabeth a final hug and a farewell kiss.[28] Mary and the other women then departed for Nazareth.

The Gift of Encouragement

Whom has God used to encourage you? Don't forget to thank them.

Is there someone whom God would want YOU to encourage this Christmas?

Think of two ways you can lift that person's spirits during December ... then do it!

Give This Gift to Others Frequently!

"And Jonathan, Saul's son, arose and went to David at Horesh and encouraged him in God" (1 Samuel 23:16).

Chapter 3
"JOSEPH, YOU MAY TAKE ONE GIANT-STEP"
(Luke 1:56; Matthew 1:18-25)

"Joseph ... do not be afraid to take Mary as your wife; for that which has been conceived in her is of the Holy Spirit" (Matthew 1:20).

Anxious to get started, Joseph interrupts Mary's thoughts. "I know you have a lot on your mind, Mary, but we really need to be on our way. We've got a long trip ahead of us."[29] Mary nods in agreement and they begin their descent into the valley.

With her experiences still fresh in her mind and her emotions so close to the surface, Mary re-lives the waves of fear that had swept over her as she walked this same stretch of road returning to Nazareth not that many weeks ago. She had been gone for more than three months visiting Elizabeth in Judea[30] and was returning home to her parents and Joseph. They were about to discover she was pregnant.[31] Mary knew God was in control of her life but she wondered if her parents and Joseph would believe her.

Mary glances over at Joseph and ponders those first, painful days of distrust, misunderstanding and uncertainty. Things had not gone well.[32] *"I can see why Joseph felt betrayed when I returned home pregnant,"* Mary thinks to herself. *"The only logical explanation for my pregnancy was that I had been unfaithful. Joseph, therefore, had every legal right and spiritual obligation to divorce me. Though deeply troubled by my pregnancy, righteous Joseph, known for extending mercy, had decided to treat me with dignity and respect.[33] In fact, just recently Joseph told me that even though he had decided to divorce me, he would have done so privately rather than shame me publicly.*

Descent to the Valley

"But then the impossible happens," Mary recalls. "Here we are on the brink of divorce, our marriage shattered by distrust, when early one morning Joseph shows up at my door. He tells me that during the night an angel appears to him in a dream.[34] The angel tells him that God is the father of my baby and instructs Joseph to complete the second stage of our marriage immediately by taking me to his house to live with him ...which is why he was there at my door that morning! Joseph's giant step of faith and obedience now protects me from accusations of adultery and makes it look like he was the one who got me pregnant. Joseph will forever be considered the father of our first child.[35]

"What family and friends do not know," Mary muses with a modest grin forming in the corners of her mouth, "is that Joseph told me he will not sleep with me until after the baby is born.[36] Joseph doesn't want there ever to be even the slightest doubt that God, not he, was responsible for my pregnancy!"

The Gift of a Healed Heart

On the brink of divorce this Christmas? Things look hopeless? Finding it difficult to forgive someone, to treat someone with dignity and respect, or to give someone a second chance? Ask God to help you love **others** the way He loves **you**!

Give This Gift to Others Unconditionally!

"But while he was still a long way off, his father saw him, and felt compassion for him, and ran and embraced him and kissed him and said, ... 'Quickly bring out the best robe and put it on him, and put a ring on his hand and sandals on his feet; and bring the fattened calf, kill it and let us eat and be merry ...'" (Luke 15:20, 22-23).

Chapter 4
"IT'S BEST WE GET OUT OF TOWN"
(Luke 2:1-4)

"And all were proceeding to register for the census" (Luke 2:3).

There are only a few other travelers as Joseph and Mary make their way down the rather steep incline. Mary, however, doesn't even notice. She is still deep in thought and memories keep flooding her mind.

When Mary had arrived back in Nazareth the city was abuzz. Caesar Augustus had decreed that a census be taken. In fact, a courier from Quirenius, governor of Syria, had personally come to Nazareth to make the announcement.[37] Riding one of the governor's black stallions, the messenger had read the proclamation throughout the city.[38] "Everyone is to return to their family's hometown to register their family's names and pay taxes on their family's land,"[39] the edict read.

Some with long distances to travel had already taken off by the time Mary arrived home. Others were planning to leave soon just to get it over with. Actually, there was no need for urgency. No deadline had been set. Caesar was far more concerned about the money than the timing.[40] Realistically, Caesar knew that because the Roman Empire was so large, the registration process would take years to complete.

Lost for a moment in her private world, Mary thoughtfully reflects. *"For Joseph and me, God's timing couldn't be better. The census gives us the perfect reason to be out of town for the remainder of my pregnancy, which*

Edict from Caesar

should eliminate questions that surely would have come up had we decided to postpone this trip until after the baby was born.[41]

"More important to Joseph than the potential gossip in Nazareth, however," Mary recalls as she pushes aside a low-hanging branch, "*were the health and safety of the baby and me. Joseph wanted to be sure I could travel that distance and that I was okay with having my first baby so far from home. Thankfully, the women helped me convince Joseph that I could make the trip to Bethlehem without unusual risk,*[42] *and once we got to Bethlehem, relatives would take care of us and help me with the delivery.*"[43]

Mary can hear the sure-footed hooves of the donkey finding their way down the hardened path. She watches the birds flitting to and fro and listens to them as they warn each other of danger. In the distance, several roosters can still be heard confidently announcing a new day. And from somewhere out of sight, a donkey erupts into what seems like an endless bray. Aware of her surroundings and amazed by the beauty and diversity of God's creation, Mary is confident that the God who causes the sun to rise in a burst of color and cares for the birds and animals that fill the earth, will watch over Joseph and her in the weeks and months to come.

The Gift of Protection

Ask God to bring into your life this Christmas a person who needs someone to defend him/her against misunderstanding, criticism, false accusation, prejudice or injustice.

Give This Gift to Others Courageously!

"Vindicate the weak and fatherless; do justice to the afflicted and destitute" (Psalm 82:3).

"Open your mouth for those who are dumb [who have no voice], for the rights of all the unfortunate. Open your mouth, judge righteously, and defend the rights of the afflicted and the needy" (Proverbs 31:8,9).

Chapter 5
"WHERE IN THE WORLD IS BETH-LEHEM?"
(Luke 2:1-5)

"And Joseph also went up from Galilee ... to the city of David, which is called Bethlehem ..." (Luke 2:4).

With the hills of Galilee behind them, Mary and Joseph head out across the valley. The sun begins to break through the morning haze, casting its soft, yellow rays on the fertile fields. The flat farmland of the Jezreel Valley makes for easy travel. Joseph leads the donkey that is carrying the provisions for the trip. Mary walks beside Joseph, allowing them to talk from time to time as they travel. Mary did a lot of walking back in Nazareth.[44]

About half way across the valley, Joseph and the donkey stop.[45]

"I think we'll go straight up here," Joseph comments to Mary as he points to the divided road ahead.[46] "It would be nice if we could head east and travel down the Jordan Valley all the way to Jericho. However, the steep climb from Jericho to Jerusalem, the stifling heat and the danger of thieves in the Judean wilderness make that route a bit too risky."[47]

As Mary and Joseph continue their journey south, they talk about the trip ahead of them.

"Traveling through Samaria is always a bit of a challenge," observes Mary, who recently traveled this same route to visit Elizabeth and Zacharias. "The road can get pretty steep and the Samaritans are not always friendly."[48]

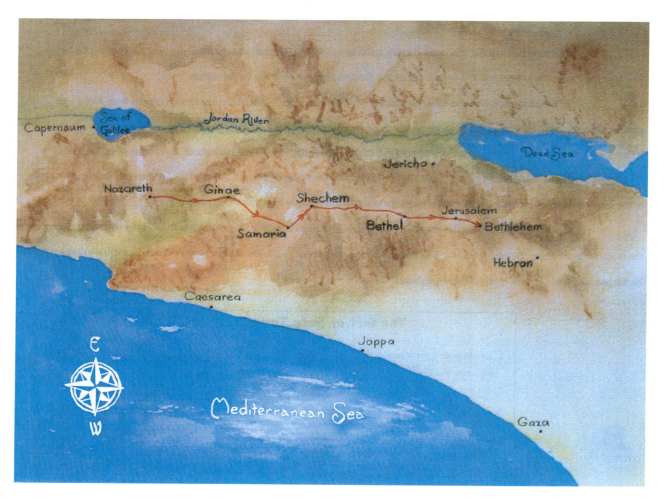

Trip to Bethlehem

"The good news is that this is the shortest route to Bethlehem," Joseph adds encouragingly. "And not too far beyond Shechem, the road starts to level out and we can follow the mountain ridge all the way to Jerusalem."

For the next week, Mary and Joseph journey toward Bethlehem.[49] Friends returning to Nazareth from Judea are greeted along the way and word of Mary and Joseph's well being is sent back to their families. Each night, Mary and Joseph and their fellow travelers camp near a spring on the outskirts of one of the many villages scattered throughout the countryside. There the animals are watered, the leather water jugs filled and a meal prepared over an open fire.[50] After a full day's travel, sleep comes easily to the weary travelers who sleep on the ground under the stars, cushioned only by a thin woven mat.

Arriving in Jerusalem in the late afternoon, Mary and Joseph decide to stay on the outskirts of the city and sleep under the stars one more night. Bethlehem is now less than a half-day's walk away.[51] They will have plenty of time tomorrow to get to Bethlehem and settle in with relatives before nightfall.[52]

The Gift of Safe Travel

Commit your Christmas schedule and travel plans to the Lord. After the holidays, thank God for His sovereign direction, protection and timing.

Receive This Gift from God Repeatedly!

"The LORD will guard your going out and your coming in from this time forth and forever" (Psalm 121:8).

Chapter 6
"NUESTRA CASA ES SU CASA"

("Our House Is Your House")

(Luke 2:6-7)

"She laid him in a feed trough because the guest room was occupied" (Luke 2:7, free translation).

After a little more than a week of travel, Mary and Joseph finally see Bethlehem in the distance. Nestled amid the rolling hills of Judea, Bethlehem is a welcome sight.[53]

Since keeping guests, especially relatives, is a cultural expectation and common courtesy in Palestine, Mary and Joseph plan to stay with family.[54] It is not uncommon for homes to have attached (either to the main level of the house or up on their flat roofs) a guest room for visitors. Mary and Joseph are hoping a guest room is available.[55]

Joseph's relatives in Bethlehem welcome him and Mary with traditional hugs and kisses. Rueben, Joseph's cousin, and his wife, Deborah, are especially excited about the pending arrival of Mary and Joseph's baby. Although their house is humble and their guest room already occupied, Rueben and Deborah insist that Mary and Joseph stay with them. Joseph and Mary are grateful for Rueben and Deborah's hospitality.

Reuben's house is like many homes. The living quarters consist of one large room. There is not much privacy.[56] The room is elevated about four feet and has a solid dirt floor. Inside the front entrance is a stable where the animals are bedded down[57] and secured nightly. During the cold months, the animals' body heat

Stable in the House

helps keep the house warm. Each morning, the animals are taken out to be watered and to graze. The stable is cleaned thoroughly for general use throughout the day.[58]

The house is entered through the stable. The elevated room is then reached by walking up several steps. Built into the raised floor of the terraced living quarters, along the border with the stable, are several feed troughs for the animals. Reuben's guest room is located on the roof of the house.

With the baby's arrival several months off and with no intention of returning to Nazareth until after the baby is born, Mary and Joseph know they will not be traveling any time soon. Joseph uses his carpentry skills to help Reuben and his neighbors. Mary spends her days going to the market with Deborah, washing clothes and cooking.[59]

The Gift of Family

God in His sovereignty has placed you into a family, which has blessed you and shaped you through both positive and negative experiences. Thank God for your biological parents as well as, perhaps, your adoptive or foster parents. Jesus was profoundly influenced by His non-biological father, Joseph. Thank God for your relatives. Proudly represent your family name. Ask God to help you continue, or perhaps by His Grace BEGIN, a godly legacy for future generations.

Accept This Gift from God Gratefully!

"God established a testimony ... and ... a law in Israel, which He commanded our fathers, that they should teach them to their children, that the generation to come might know, even the children yet to be born, that they may arise and tell them to their children, that they should put their confidence in God, and not forget the works of God, but keep His commandments" (Psalm 77:5-7).

Chapter 7
SPECIAL DELIVERY
(Luke 2:6-7)

"She gave birth to her first-born son; and she wrapped Him in cloths, and laid Him in a manger" (Luke 2:7).

As the unsuspecting town of Bethlehem goes about its business, Mary goes into labor.[60] It is nearly mid-morning and Mary and Deborah have no more than returned from the market when the contractions begin. By late afternoon, the contractions are quite frequent and severe. Deborah and a local midwife assist Mary with the delivery.[61] The baby is born in the early evening.[62]

"It's a boy," announces the midwife.

Mary is tempted to say, "I know," but decides the explanation is far too complicated for the moment.

The news of the safe delivery is immediately relayed to Joseph who is sitting outside with Reuben, the other houseguests, and several neighbors. They have already heard the baby cry but appreciate the assurance that Mary and the baby are fine.

The traditional cloth wrappings for newborns have already been prepared by Mary and Deborah. After washing the baby and rubbing him with salt, Mary tenderly wraps her baby boy in the strips of cloth.[63]

When things are put in order and Mary is resting comfortably, Joseph and Reuben enter the house. Reuben lets Joseph take the lead as they walk up the short flight of stairs. All eyes are on the baby cradled in Mary's arms.

Birth of Jesus

As Joseph approaches Mary, Mary lifts her head and looks deeply into Joseph's eyes. They are in this together. They will need each other in the months and years ahead.

Mary and Joseph exchange smiles of relief and joy as Joseph leans over, embraces Mary, and kisses her forehead. He then lays his hand on his son and quietly whispers, "Blessed be this child. Blessed be his mother. Thanks be to God!"[64]

A feed trough is transformed into a crib. The hollowed out trough is cleaned and carefully lined with sheepskin. The baby is gently laid in the feed trough.[65]

Mary rests while Deborah prepares the evening meal.

The Gifts of Life and Individuality

God has uniquely made you for His glory. Ask God to help you be content with how He created you. Thank God for your birth parents. Think of a creative way this Christmas to thank your parents for giving you the gift of life.

Embrace These Gifts from God Unashamedly!

"For Thou didst form my inward parts; Thou didst weave me together in my mother's womb. I will give thanks to Thee, for I am fearfully and wonderfully made" (Psalm 139:13-14).

Chapter 8

THE SCAVENGER HUNT

(Luke 2:15-16)

"And they came in haste and found their way to Mary and Joseph, and the baby" (Luke 2:16).

After supper, Mary, Joseph, Reuben, Deborah, and other family members who have come to see the baby relate stories and rehearse God's faithfulness. Joseph is especially thankful to God for his generous relatives who are willing to share what little they have with him and his family.

As the guests prepare to leave and Mary is about to get some much-needed sleep, voices are heard outside and there is a knock at the door. Reuben goes to see who is there. When he opens the door, he is greeted by a group of excited shepherds. Reuben does not know all of them by name, but is familiar with most of their families.[66]

Before Reuben even has a chance to ask the shepherds why they have come, the shepherd closest to him asks, "Was a baby born here today? We've been asking all over town about the birth of a baby. One of the market ladies told us that your visitors were expecting their baby to be born any day now."[67]

"Yes," Reuben responds. "Earlier this evening our relative, Mary, gave birth to a baby boy."

Reuben invites the shepherds in.

As the shepherds enter the house, there, right in front of them is a baby wrapped in cloths, lying in a feed trough, just as they had been told.[68] The shepherds are amazed! They had found what they were searching for!

Visit of the Shepherds

Caught up in the excitement of the moment, the shepherds, half in awe, half in bewilderment, talk among themselves. Those in the house strain to hear what the shepherds are saying.[69]

Suddenly realizing their rudeness, one of the shepherds turns to those in the house and says, "You won't believe whom God sent to us out in the fields tonight to tell us about this little baby!"

The Gift of Special Revelation

Thank God that He has let us know what He is up to in the world. Thank God for the Bible, the written Word, and for Jesus, the Living Word.
Consider reading through the entire Bible this coming year.

Consult This Gift from God Daily!

"He made known His ways to Moses, His acts to the sons of Israel" (Psalm 103:7). "Surely the LORD God does nothing unless He reveals His secret counsel to His servants the prophets" (Amos 3:7).

"God, after He spoke long ago to the fathers in the prophets in many portions and in many ways, in these last days has spoken to us in His Son ..." (Hebrews 1:1-2).

Chapter 9
THE ORIGINAL HALLELUJAH CHORUS
(Luke 2:8-20)

"And suddenly there appeared with the angel a multitude of the heavenly host praising God..." (Luke 2:13).

Everyone in the house is anxious to hear how this excited group of local shepherds came to know about the birth of Mary and Joseph's son, and why they so quickly searched to find him.

"Did God send you a prophet?" Reuben finally ventures in response to the shepherd's question.

"No," replies the shepherd. "But tonight, my friends and I were with our sheep on a hill outside of Bethlehem just like every other night. It was dark and we were talking about the events of the day. Then suddenly, a dazzling angel appeared right there in front of us and a brilliant light almost blinded us! We were terrified!

"The angel," explains the shepherd, "calmly spoke to us and said, 'Do not be afraid. For behold, I bring you good news of great joy, which shall be for all the people. For today in the city of David, there has been born for you a Savior, who is Christ the Lord. And this will be a sign for you. You will find a baby wrapped in cloths, and lying in a feed trough.'"[70]

"If that wasn't enough," another shepherd blurts out, "and I know you won't believe this, out of no where, thousands upon thousands of angels lit up the night sky. They praised God and said, 'Glory to God in the highest, and on earth peace among men with whom He is pleased.'[71] Then, just as suddenly, everything was dark and quiet! It happened so fast it hardly seemed real!"

Dazzled by an Angel

"Which is why we decided to come into town," yet another shepherd adds. "We wanted to see if we could find this baby the angel told us about. That's why we're here!"[72]

All those in the house are amazed at the shepherds' story. Mary, however, is particularly intrigued by their words. Slowly but surely, God is revealing to her His divine purpose for her life and the significance of her son.[73]

Having found the baby and having told their story, the shepherds return to the hills outside of Bethlehem to care for their sheep. As they go, like the angels, they glorify and praise God for all that they have heard and seen. Everything turned out to be just like the angel had said.[74]

The Gift of Praise

For what life experience of this past year does your heart overflow with praise? Let that praise overflow to others.

Give This Gift to God and Others Spontaneously!

"Through Him then, let us continually offer up a sacrifice of praise to God, that is, the fruit of lips that give thanks to His name" (Hebrews 13:15).

Chapter 10
LAW-ABIDING CITIZENS
(Luke 2:21-38; Matthew 1:25)

"And when the eight days were completed before His circumcision, His name was then called Jesus ... And when their days of purification ...were complete, they brought Him up to Jerusalem to be presented to the Lord" (Luke 2:21-22).

A week after the baby is born, he is circumcised as commanded in the Law of Moses[75] and given a name. The angel had told Joseph in a dream to name the baby *Jesus* because he would save his people from their sins. Mary had also been told by Gabriel that the baby was to be named *Jesus*. Mary and Joseph are in complete agreement. The baby is named *Jesus*.[76]

Over the next five weeks, Mary completes the forty days of purification as the Law of Moses requires for the birth of a son.[77] Merely completing the required days, however, is not sufficient according to Moses' Law. To openly celebrate the completion of this requirement, to visually atone for a woman's uncleanness and to officially and publicly declare that the woman who had the baby is now clean and again able to participate in the on-going religious life of the nation of Israel, the new mother is required to go to the Temple in Jerusalem and present two sacrifices to the Lord—a burnt offering and a sin offering.[78] The burnt offering is normally a one-year-old lamb. The Law does allow for the substitution of a pigeon or a young turtledove if the mother cannot afford a lamb.

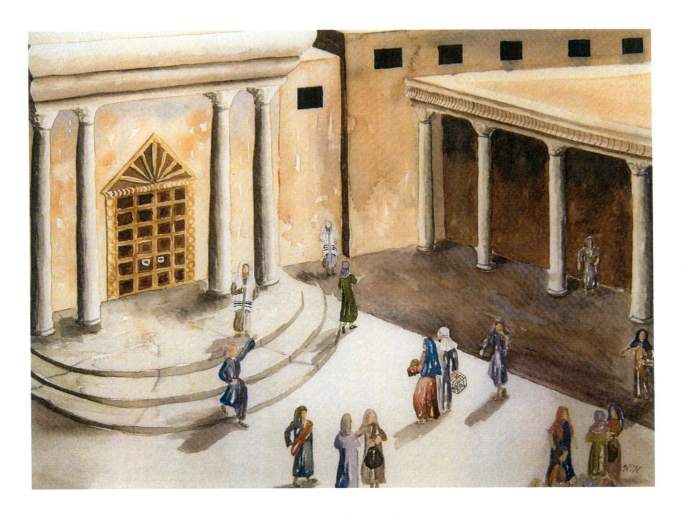

Visit to the Temple

When Mary's days of purification are complete, therefore, she and Joseph travel up to Jerusalem.[79] They leave Bethlehem early in the morning so they can be back before dark. Because Mary cannot afford a lamb, she takes two turtledoves for the sacrifices. Mary presents the birds to the priest at the doorway of the Temple.[80]

After Mary is declared to be clean, Mary and Joseph present Baby Jesus to the Lord[81] and pay the five-shekel redemption price for firstborn sons.[82] This ransom payment had been instituted by God after Israel's exodus from Egypt.[83] Mary and Joseph find great satisfaction in obediently fulfilling the requirements of God's Law.[84]

The Gift of Stewardship

This Christmas, take some time to again acknowledge that all you have, including your children, belong to God. With opened hands stretched out before God, give everything back to God. Tell Him that you will not tightly hold on to those things that by His grace He has given you to care for on His behalf during your short time here on Planet Earth.

Administrate This Gift from God Faithfully!

"A certain nobleman went to a distant country to receive a kingdom for himself and then return. And he called his ten slaves, and gave them ten minas, and said to them, 'Do business with this until I come back'" (Luke 19:12-13).

Chapter 11
TWO PROPHETS AND A BABY
(Luke 2:25-38)

"There was a man in Jerusalem whose name was Simeon. And there was a prophetess, Anna, the daughter of Phanuel" (Luke 2:25, 36).

Mary and Joseph are ready to leave the Temple when suddenly, an elderly man approaches them. "I am Simeon," the man states, "a servant of the God of Israel. Some time ago, the Holy Spirit revealed to me that I would not die before seeing the Lord's Anointed—the Christ. May I hold your child?"

"Of course," replies Mary, handing Baby Jesus to Simeon.

Cradling Baby Jesus in his arms, Simeon blesses God and says, "Lord, I am your servant, and now I can die in peace, because you have kept your promise to me. With my own eyes I have seen what you have done to save your people, and foreign nations will also see this. Your mighty power is a light for all nations, and it will bring honor to your people Israel."[85]

Simeon hands Baby Jesus back to Mary and Joseph and blesses them. He then says to Mary, "This child of yours will cause many people in Israel to fall and others to stand. The child will be like a warning sign. Many people will reject him, and you, Mary, will suffer as though you had been stabbed by a dagger."[86]

Isaiah had prophesied that Israel would reject their Messiah and put Him to death.[87] God, however, would change that curse into a blessing.[88] With Mary looking on at Golgotha, Jesus, fully God and fully

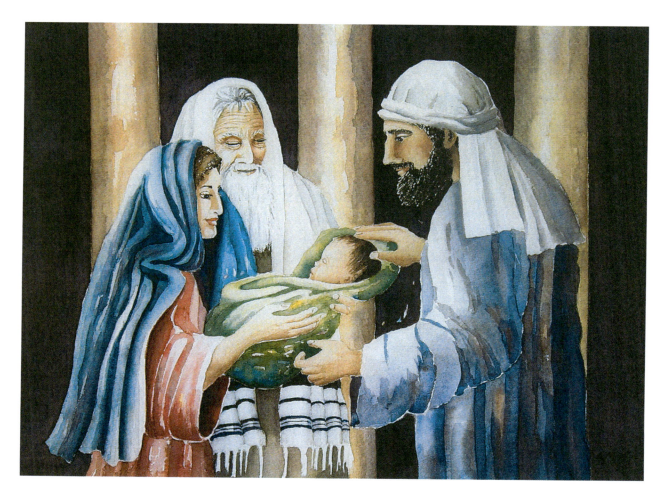

Encounter with Simeon

human, would shed his blood and die on the cross. As the sinless *Passover lamb*,[89] Jesus would bear the sins *of* and pay sin's penalty *for* all humanity,[90] so that whoever would believe in Jesus as the divine sin-bearer and follow Him, would not go to hell, but have everlasting life.[91] God would show that He accepted Jesus' death on the cross as payment for humanity's sin by raising Jesus from the dead.[92]

No more has Simeon finished his prayers of blessing and prophecy than an 84-year-old widow named Anna, a prophetess who has served night and day in the Temple most of her adult life, comes up to Mary and Joseph and gives thanks to God. She explains to all those in the Temple how important a role this baby boy, Jesus, will play in the future redemption of Jerusalem.[93]

Mary and Joseph are intrigued by the words of Simeon and Anna. All the way back to Bethlehem, they talk about their unexpected experiences in the Temple and the dramatic statements made concerning their son.

The Gift of Affirmation

Thoughtfully prepare an individualized blessing for your spouse and each of your children and/or grandchildren. Capture in figurative language qualities in their lives that you believe God has given them to be a blessing to others. Then, in a family setting, pronounce that blessing upon each one of them.[94]

Give This Gift to Your Family Intentionally!

"Then Jacob summoned his sons and said, 'Assemble yourselves that I may tell you what shall befall you in the days to come'" (Genesis 49:1).

Chapter 12

FOR GOD SO LOVED THE "WISE GUYS"

(Matthew 2:11)

"And they came into the house and saw the Child with Mary His mother" (Matthew 2:11).

With the registration and taxation completed, the baby delivered, the circumcision performed, the baby named, the purification sacrifices offered, and the redemption payment for first-born sons made, Mary and Joseph are ready to return to Nazareth.[95]

Only days before their planned return home, however, Mary and Joseph are visiting with Reuben and Deborah in their house one evening[96] when they again hear voices outside and a knock at the door. Reuben gets up and goes to the door. After a muffled discussion, Reuben invites the visitors in.

Mary, Joseph, and Deborah are startled when they see five men enter the house.[97] The visitors are strangely dressed. They are clearly from one of the countries to the east. The men appear wealthy and well educated.

The visitors politely greet Joseph, Mary, and Deborah. The foreigners speak Greek just like the residents of Bethlehem. Their accent, however, makes them somewhat difficult to understand. When the foreigners see the baby in the arms of Mary, they bow down in the stable and worship him.

Reuben invites the visitors up the stairs to join the family in the living quarters. Once they are comfortably seated, Rueben and Joseph bring them water to wash their feet. Deborah and Mary give the guests something to drink, then quietly exit to get some additional food from the neighbors. A meal is quickly prepared for the strangers.[98]

Arrival of Foreigners

The Gift of Cultural Diversity

Think of someone from another culture or sub-culture that God has used to bless you. Take time to thank them. Now think of someone from a culture or sub-culture who is so different that you cannot imagine them a follower of Jesus. Unconditionally love them, genuinely befriend them and regularly pray for them.

Receive This Gift from God Humbly!

"There came a woman from Samaria to draw water. Jesus said to her, 'Give Me a drink.' The Samaritan woman therefore said to Him, 'How is it that You, being a Jew ask me for a drink since I am a Samaritan woman?' (For Jews have no dealings with Samaritans)" (John 4:7, 9).

And as they were coming out [of Jerusalem], they found a man of Cyrene named Simon, whom they pressed into service to bear His cross" (Matthew 27:32).

"For He Himself is our peace who made both groups into one, and broke down the barrier of the dividing wall ..." (Ephesians 2:14).

Chapter 13

STAR TREK

(Matthew 2:1-10)

"And lo, the star, which they had seen in the east, went on before them" (Matthew 2:9).

After the guests are fed and their animals and servants attended to, the apparent leader of the group relates to those in the house why they have come.[99]

"We are wise men from the East," the foreigner begins.[100] "We study the stars. About two years ago a new star appeared in our night skies to the West. It was unlike anything we had ever seen! The nightly spectacle continued month after month and we spent long hours discussing what the significance of the star might be.

"Because we believe unusual stars are linked to the birth of kings," the wise man explains, "and because we knew your sacred writings spoke of the birth of a coming king, we concluded that your long-awaited king might have been born. We therefore prepared some gifts and left for Jerusalem, your nation's ancient capital.[101]

"After traveling almost four weeks,[102] we finally arrived in Jerusalem and began asking people if they knew about the birth of the King of the Jews. We explained to them that we had seen his star back in our country and had come to worship him.[103]

"When King Herod heard about us and our search," the wise man adds, obviously pleased with the attention Herod had given them, "he asked the Jews' chief priests and scribes if they knew anything about the

Bathed in Starlight

birth of such a baby. The Jewish leaders told Herod that their prophets of old had in fact predicted the coming of a future Messiah King who would be born in the town of Bethlehem.[104]

"Having confirmed your ancient prophecy, King Herod met with us in private and asked us how long it had been since we first saw the star. We were more than willing to tell him. The king then asked us to let him know immediately once we located the baby so he could also come and worship him.[105] With that, King Herod sent us on our way.

"However, we no more than left Jerusalem for Bethlehem," the wise man exclaims with renewed excitement, "than that unusual star which had appeared in our night skies for the past two years suddenly reappears in front of us![106] We could hardly believe our eyes! The star appears to be near yet far, distant yet close, as it hangs suspended above the treetops. Amazed, we followed the star as it moved southward, lighting the road in front of us. Arriving in Bethlehem the star led us through town until it finally stopped right above your house, bathing your home in starlight![107] That is why we knocked at your door. That is why we bowed and worshipped this child."

The Gift of Divine Guidance

Reflect on how God has led you throughout your life. Thank God for His guidance. Be ready to share your life experiences with someone seeking God's direction.

Share This Gift with Others Openly!

"Trust in the LORD with all your heart, and do not lean on your own understanding. In all your ways acknowledge Him, and He will make your paths straight" (Proverbs 3:5-6).

Chapter 14

PAY IT FORWARD

(Matthew 2:11-12)

"And opening their treasures, they presented to Him gifts of gold and frankincense and myrrh" (Matthew. 2:11).

Their fascinating story told, the visitors get up, return to their camels, and enter moments later with several saddlebags. The wise men walk up the stairs to the living area, take out numerous bundles, and carefully unwrap their treasured gifts—gold, frankincense, and myrrh.[108] They reverently set the gifts on the floor in front of Mary and Baby Jesus, then bow and worship the King of the Jews.[109] Neither the wise men nor Mary and Joseph understand at the moment just how important these gifts will be as God's provision for Mary and Joseph in the coming months.

With the hour now late, Reuben invites the visitors to bring in their bedrolls and settle in for the night. The members of the household do the same. Some sleep under the stars up on the roof. Others sleep inside the house. Soon all are comfortable. Virtually all the available space is covered with bedrolls.[110]

The guests will only stay one night. They have found what they were looking for and have accomplished what they set out to do.

An oil lamp in the corner dimly lights the room.

The guests are up early the next morning, anxious to be on their way. During the night, however, God has spoken to one of the wise men in a dream, telling him that they are not to return to King Herod but are to return home a different way.

Giving of Gifts

While the camels are readied for the trip, the visitors exchange customary words of farewell and gratitude with their hosts, Rueben and Deborah, as well as with Joseph and Mary. To avoid Jerusalem, the wise men go south toward Hebron before connecting with a road that takes them west out of the Judean hills. From there, they follow the trade route north all the way home.[111] By God's grace, these God-fearing foreigners had been among the first to worship Jesus, King of the Jews and Savior of the world!

With the foreigners gone and the drama of the past twenty-four hours over, Mary and Joseph are overwhelmed by all that God has revealed to them in recent months about their son and by all those God has used as His messengers. First it was the angel Gabriel, then Elizabeth and Zacharias, then the shepherds and their story about the angels, then Simeon, then Anna, and now these Gentile astrologers and their fascination with a star! The story, however, is far from over for Mary and Joseph.

The Gift of Timely Provision

Review, personally or as a family, how over the years God has provided for your needs in ordinary and extraordinary ways.

Might there be someone with a special need this Christmas for whom God wants to provide through YOU?

Instead of exchanging gifts this year, might God want you to use that money to help someone in need?

Give This Gift to Others Prayerfully!

"Then Abraham raised his eyes and looked, and behold, behind him a ram caught in the thicket by his horns; and Abraham went and took the ram and offered him for a burnt offering in the place of his son. And Abraham called the name of that place The LORD Will Provide [Yahweh-jireh], as it is said to this day, "'In the mount of the LORD it will be provided'" (Genesis 22:13-14).

Chapter 15
MURDER, HE WROTE
(Matthew 2:13-18; Luke 2:39)

"Arise and take the Child and His mother, and flee to Egypt" (Matthew 2:13).

Within days of the wise men's departure, an angel of the Lord appears to Joseph in a dream and says, "Arise and take the Child and His mother, and flee to Egypt, and remain there until I tell you; for Herod is going to search for the Child to destroy Him."[112]

The startling dream awakens Joseph. And although it is the middle of the night, he immediately does what the angel told him to do.

Joseph begins by waking up Mary, Reuben, and Deborah. He then loads their few belongings and the gifts from the wise men onto the donkey. Finally, after thanking Reuben and Deborah for their hospitality and saying good-bye, Mary, Joseph, and Baby Jesus depart for Egypt under the cloak of darkness.[113]

Mary and Joseph leave none too soon. King Herod has realized that the wise men have ignored his request. Angry, and fearful of losing his kingdom to a potential political rival, King Herod, according to the time the wise men told him the star first appeared, orders all baby boys two years old and younger to be killed in Bethlehem and the surrounding area.[114]

Joseph, Mary and Baby Jesus travel south out of Bethlehem to Hebron.[115] From there they leave the Judean hills, traveling south to Egypt on the coastal trade route. The trip takes them several weeks. Although the trip is difficult for Mary and Joseph and the Infant Jesus, God gives them strength and protection as they

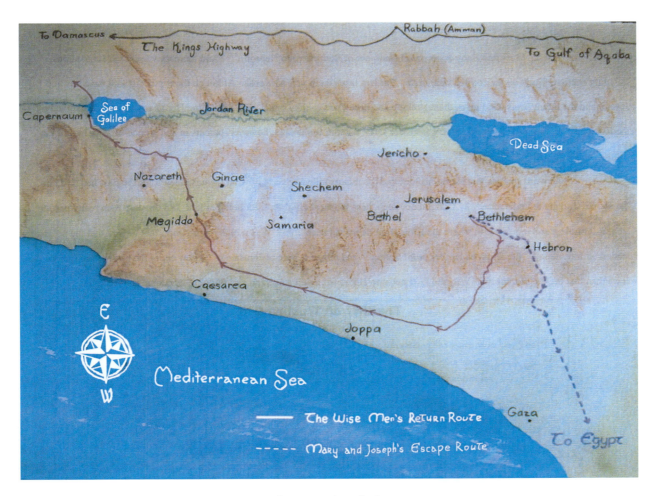

Change in Travel Plans

travel. Far from King Herod and in a land governed by the Roman Empire, Mary, Joseph and Baby Jesus are safe. Back in Bethlehem, however, parents in and around the city mourn the death of their martyred infants.

As word spreads that Herod had ordered the infants killed because of what the wise men from the East had told him, the people struggle to understand why God did not keep these innocent children from being killed. Did the wise men really need to stop in Jerusalem and inquire as to where the King of the Jews had been born? Was it really more important to God that the political leaders in Jerusalem,[116] the religious leaders in Jerusalem,[117] and all the people of Jerusalem[118] know about the birth of the King of the Jews than that these children live? Why did God not stop Herod from doing such an evil thing? The people are sad and confused.

The Gift of Trusting God

Has God ever physically spared your life? Has God ever allowed tragedy to strike your family? Ask God to give you an opportunity this Christmas to share with someone how your relationship with Christ helps you trust the goodness of God in both the good times and bad, even when you don't understand His ways.

Share This Gift with Others Humbly and Reverently

"... always being ready to make a defense to everyone who asks you to give an account for the hope that is in you, yet with gentleness and reverence" (1 Peter 3:15).

Chapter 16
"ARE WE THERE YET?"
(Luke 2:19-23)

"Arise and take the Child and His mother, and go into the land of Israel" (Matthew 2:20).

Joseph's plan was only to go as far south as Bethlehem and to stay there only until duly registered and the baby was born. God's timing and geographical will for Joseph and his family's lives, however, were different. Like Joseph of Old Testament fame, Joseph and Mary suddenly find themselves in Egypt where they are to remain until the angel of the Lord tells them they can return.[119]

For the next couple of years, God is silent. Day after day, however, God faithfully provides for Mary and Joseph's needs. Mary and Joseph are thankful to God for the wise men's gifts of gold, frankincense, and myrrh.

Finally, in God's time, King Herod dies. It is now safe for the Child Jesus to return to Galilee where, by this time, Mary's pregnancy is a distant memory to the people of Nazareth. God suddenly breaks His silence.

One night while Joseph is sleeping, the angel of the Lord appears to him in a dream, saying, "Arise and take the Child and His mother, and go into the land of Israel; for those who sought the Child's life are dead."[120]

Mary and Joseph are excited about returning to Palestine. They have longed to see their families and to show them their baby boy. They quickly pack up their belongings and leave for the land of Israel.

Home at Last!

Because the hill country of Judea is only slightly out of the way, Mary and Joseph plan to visit Zacharias, Elizabeth, Reuben, and Deborah on their way back to Nazareth. However, when Joseph hears that King Herod's son, Archelaus, is reigning over Judea, Joseph decides not to go through Bethlehem and Jerusalem on their way north. God confirms Joseph's fears and warns him through yet another dream to avoid Judea.[121] Mary and Joseph continue north on the main trade route along the costal plain.

After weeks of travel, Joseph and the family make their way through the Megiddo Pass, across the Jezreel Valley, and up the winding road to Nazareth.[122] At the top of the high hill, Joseph, Mary and Jesus turn and look back across the valley. The late afternoon sun hangs like a piece of ripe fruit in the Western sky and shadows lengthen as the sun begins to slip behind the Mountains of Carmel. It has been quite a trip!

When Mary and Joseph left Nazareth, they had no idea that their obedience to God would lead them all the way to Egypt and back. God, however, had been faithful each literal step of the way. His fingerprints were all over Jesus' birth. God had led them, encouraged them, provided for them, and protected them at every turn. Mary and Joseph know they can trust their Heavenly Father through whatever lies ahead.

As the sun sets and stars without number fill the sky, what Mary and Joseph do not fully understand is that their son, Jesus, peacefully sleeping in the other room, created them all.

The Gift of God's Faithfulness

Share with someone how God faithfully brought you through a particularly stressful time in your life and how that experience strengthened your faith and trust in your Heavenly Father.

Be Inspired by This Gift and Share It with Others Continually!

"The LORD's lovingkindnesses indeed never cease, for His compassions never fail. They are new every morning; great is Thy faithfulness" (Lamentations 3:22-23).

CREATOR CHRIST
HOW GREAT THOU ART

All things were made by Him, and without Him nothing was made that was made (John 1:3).
For by Him all things were created—all things have been created by Him and for Him (Colossians 1:16).
God . . . has spoken to us in His Son . . . through whom also He made the world (Heb. 1:1-3).

Jesus, My Lord, I read the Christmas story,
And stand amazed by Your great love for me.
You traded heav'n, Your power and Your glory,
For Mary's womb, in meek humility.

(chorus)
My heart cries out, Creator Christ to Thee,
"How great Thou art! How great Thou art!"
My heart cries out, Jesus of Galilee,
"How great Thou art! How great Thou art!"

Can't comprehend, how You, the Great Creator,
Hurled into space a million galaxies.
Then became flesh—a baby, born of Mary,
So You could die for all humanity.

You taught us how to love by serving others.
Multiplied bread. Changed water into wine.
You calmed the sea. Washed feet. Cleansed outcast lepers.
Your works and words declared You were divine.

What boundless love, You let creation kill You.
Nailed to a cross. Displayed for all to see.
Metal and wood fettered Your hands of mercy.
With outstretched arms, You died to set us free.

When You return and free all of creation,
Sin, sorrow, death will finally pass away.
And just as wise men worshipped Baby Jesus,
With hearts of joy, we'll praise You, and we'll say: (chorus)

- Jared Burkholder, December 2006
- Musical setting: *How Great Thou Art*

ENDNOTES

Insights into the biblical text, history, culture, and geography

CHAPTER 1

[1] (p 2) Nazareth (elevation: 1,320 ft.) sits on the southern ridge of the hills of Lower Galilee. The city overlooks the Jezreel Valley which is slightly above sea level.

Nazareth's geography plays a prominent role in the history of Jesus' life. Jesus returns to the synagogue in Nazareth and reads from the Old Testament Scriptures. After claiming that He, that day, is fulfilling the passage just read, Jesus goes on to praise the faith of two Gentiles in the Old Testament—that of the widow of Zarephath and that of Naaman the Syrian (Lk 4:16-27). Luke then adds, *"And all in the synagogue were filled with rage as they heard these things; and they rose up and cast Him out of the city, and led Him to the brow of the hill* [overlooking the Jezreel Valley] *on which their city had been built, in order to throw Him down the cliff. But passing through their midst, He went His way"* (Lk 4:28-30).

[2] (p 2) The biblical text gives no clue as to the ages of Mary and Joseph. Mary is perhaps as young as 15 but could easily be in her late teens or early twenties. Wilkins notes, "Young men and women were often pledged between twelve and thirteen years of age, although later rabbinic texts suggest that men in Jesus' day often married around the age of eighteen" (Wilkins 2004, 73).

[3] (p 2) Although the biblical text does not specify how soon after Gabriel's announcement to Mary she becomes pregnant, the historical sequence of events, the time references indicated in the text, and some simple math calculations, help us develop a general timeline.

Three biblical statements provide the framework for our understanding. First, Gabriel tells Mary that Elizabeth *"is now in her sixth month"* [i.e., a little over five months pregnant] (Lk 1:36). Secondly, when Mary arrives at Elizabeth's home, John the Baptist leaps in Elizabeth's womb apparently at the presence of the Messiah in Mary's womb (Lk 1:39-44). Thirdly, Mary returns to Nazareth before Elizabeth gives birth to John the Baptist (Lk 1:56-57). These interesting facts recorded by Dr. Luke suggest the following timetable: (1) Mary becomes pregnant almost immediately after Gabriel's visit; (2) Mary leaves to visit Elizabeth within a week or two of Gabriel's appearance ["*Mary arose and <u>went with haste</u> to the hill country, to a city of Judah*" (Lk 1:39, emphasis added)]; and (3) after a week or so of travel, Mary arrives at Elizabeth's house two to three weeks pregnant.

If Mary arrives at Elizabeth's home two-three weeks pregnant, stays with Elizabeth "*about three months*" (Lk 1:56), then travels home for another week, Mary arrives back in Nazareth three-and-a-half to four months pregnant. As will be noted later, Mary and Joseph could easily have left for Bethlehem within a month or two of Mary's return to Nazareth from Judea.

[4] (p 2) Bridewealth (sometimes referred to as the *bride price*) is the term used by cultural anthropologists to describe the financial compensation given by the family of the groom to the family of the bride to seal the marriage arrangement between their children (Ferarro 2001, 193).

[5] (p 2) In first century Palestine, marriage is an arrangement between two families more than it is an arrangement between two individuals (McHugh 1975, 158-59). The families enter into legally binding marriage commitments with respect to their children.

	Courtship	Marriage
West	Dating / Engagement	

	Family Negotiation (Arrangement)	Marriage	
		Stage 1	Stage 2
East		Betrothal	Cohabitation

Arranged marriages, therefore, consist of two stages. The first stage is called the *betrothal* or *espoused* stage. This stage begins when the families finalize their commitments. In the *betrothal* stage the couple is legally bound together though the man and woman do not live together. Release from these commitments requires a legal divorce (Mt 1:18-19; Lk 1:27; 2:5; 2 Cor 11:2).

Betrothal is a category for which we in the West have no cultural, and, therefore, no linguistic equivalent. *Betrothal* **should not** be confused with our North American concept of *engagement*. In Western society, *engagement* is a public, non-legal, highly individualistic declaration of a man and a woman that they intend to marry. *Engagement* is part of courtship, not marriage. *Betrothal*, on the other hand, though also public, is better thought of as being part of *marriage*, not courtship, and involves the families. So, while we in the West culturally think of Mary as *single and pregnant*, according to Middle Eastern culture Mary is *betrothed and pregnant*, a very different cultural dilemma.

That *betrothal* rises to the level of *marriage* is reflected in Deuteronomy 22:22-29. In that passage, instructions are given regarding sexual relations outside of *marriage*. In verse 22, the Mosaic Law declares that if a Stage 2 *married* woman commits adultery, both she and her sexual partner are to be put to death (obviously for violating the *marriage* vow). Likewise in Deuteronomy 22:23, if a Stage 1 (*betrothed*) *married* woman has sexual relations in the city limits with someone other than her husband and she does not cry out for help, both she and her sexual partner are to be put to death (presumably for that same violation of the "marriage" vow). In other words, infidelity at either stage was considered adultery, deserving death. The death penalty is not imposed, however, on a non-*betrothed* couple who has *pre-marital* sex (Deut 22:28-29; Ex 22:16-17).

The word *"engagement"*, therefore, is a confusing if not inaccurate translation of *mnesteuo*, the Greek word for *betrothal* (Vine 1996, 64) used by Luke (Lk 2:5) and Matthew (Mt 1:18) to describe the relationship between Mary and Joseph.

[6] (p 2) By this time Gabriel has already appeared to Zacharias in the Temple. Previous to that appearance, however, the last time the angel Gabriel is mentioned in Scripture is when he appears to Daniel some 500 years before (Dan 8:16; 9:21).

[7] (p 4) Luke 1:30-33.

[8] (p 4) Luke 1:34. Mary's question to Gabriel about how she could give birth to a child when she had never had sexual relations with a man brings up a topic that we are all aware of, one which no doubt has at one time or another flashed through your mind, yet one I do not remember ever having heard discussed as part of the Christmas story. I am referring, of course, to the topic of sex and the prominent role that sex and sexuality play in the Christmas story. Sexually active senior citizens who struggle with infertility and menopause, Mary's question about conceiving a baby without a man, Mary's supposed adultery, sex during

pregnancy and Joseph keeping Mary a virgin (lit. *"was not knowing her"*) until after Jesus is born assume a mature audience.

In this regard, I would note that although the Christmas story is rather consistently packaged as a children's story, amazingly, the Christmas story in the Scriptures is anything but that. Matthew and Luke write to adults, not children ... adults with a rather broad understanding physiologically about sex. Much could and should be said about the Christmas story and sex (even as it has to do with the need for the virgin birth of Christ with respect to such theological concepts such as substitutionary atonement, redemption, forgiveness, and salvation) but this is not my purpose. Suffice it to say that the church should take the initiative to dialogue with Sunday school teachers, youth leaders, and parents to explore how the church and the home can creatively capitalize upon this perfect opportunity to talk about sex and sexuality. Unfortunately, even though sex and sexuality are major themes in the Christmas story, the word sex will probably not even be heard in Christian homes or Sunday school classrooms in relation to Christmas. The Christmas story, however, holds great potential for dialoguing with youth, and even children, about sexuality.

[9] (p 4) Luke 1:34-37.
[10] (p 4) Isaiah 7:14.
[11] (p 4) Luke 1:38.

CHAPTER 2

[12] (p 6) The angel Gabriel describes in very general, non-sexual terms the process whereby Mary conceives a son. The biblical text, however, does not mention when, or where or how this happens. The text simply says, *"Now the birth of Jesus Christ was as follows. When His mother Mary had been betrothed to Joseph, before they came together she was found to be with child by the Holy Spirit"* (Mt 1:18). From the reaction of John the Bap-

tist in the womb of Elizabeth when Mary arrived at Zacharias and Elizabeth's home, it appears that John's reaction was because he was in the presence of the Messiah, already developing in Mary's womb. From the biblical text, therefore, it seems most likely that the Holy Spirit came upon Mary prior to her trip to Judea to visit Elizabeth and Zacharias. [See endnote 3, pp 62-63.]

[13] (p 6) One of the perplexing features of the Christmas story is the total absence in the biblical text of any dialogue between Mary and Joseph or between Mary and her parents with regard to Gabriel's visit, Elizabeth's pregnancy, or Mary's miraculous conception. It appears that Mary did not tell Joseph or her parents about her pregnancy. The biblical account offers no clues as to why Mary apparently told no one. [See endnotes 30-31, pp 71-72.]

[14] (p 6) *"And after these days Elizabeth, his wife, became pregnant; and she kept herself in seclusion* (lit. *hid herself* [i.e., hid her condition], from the Greek word, *perikrupto*) *for five months ..."* Lk 1:24). The word *perikrupto* "signifies to hide by placing something around, to conceal entirely, to keep hidden (*peri*, 'around,' used intensively ...)" (Vine 1996, 303). Metaphorically, Elizabeth shrouds her pregnancy in silence. Literally, Elizabeth hides her pregnancy for five months under the loose, traditional clothing that the women wear.

[15] (p 6) Though Luke 1:39 (1) makes no reference to Mary informing her parents or Joseph about Elizabeth's pregnancy, (2) gives no indication as to why Mary did not inform them, and (3) makes it sound like Mary (totally on her own) decides to go visit Elizabeth, it seems incomprehensible that Mary would have taken off without telling her parents or Joseph where she was going, why she was going, and the source of the information upon which she was going. This is especially true given her age. It is not as though we are talking about a 30-year-old single adult. We are talking about an espoused young lady who is under the authority of Joseph and her father.

[16] (p 6) While the text states, "*Mary <u>arose</u> and went <u>with haste</u> to the hill country, to a city in Judah*" (Lk 1:39, emphasis added), it is logical to assume that others accompany her. It seems highly unlikely that Mary's parents and Joseph would send her to Judea by herself. It is not uncommon for the biblical text to focus on one person, only to reveal to the reader later on that other individuals are involved.

In Genesis 24, for example, the text says, "*Then the servant* [Eliezer, Abraham's servant] *took ten camels from the camels of his master, and set out with a variety of good things of his master's in his hand; and he arose, and went to Mesopotamia, to the city of Nahor*" (Gen 24:10). Later in that passage, however, the text says, "*Then he* [Eliezer] <u>*and the men who were with him*</u> *ate and drank and spent the night*" (Gen 24:54, emphasis added).

[17] (p 6) Luke writes that Mary "*went with haste ...*" to Judea (Lk 1:39). The "*haste*" appears to be linked to the quickness of the response and to the immediacy of Mary's departure rather than to the speed with which Mary traveled.

[18] (p 6) Like the Jews in Bible times, many cultures today highly value family loyalty and often travel long distances to celebrate milestone events of relatives, such as weddings and funerals.

[19] (p 6) Luke inserts the fact that Elizabeth lives in a city in the hill country of Judea (Lk 1:39). This means that Elizabeth's town is located not that far from Jerusalem and Bethlehem. Bethlehem is some 80+ miles south of Nazareth.

The name of the Judean town where Zacharias and Elizabeth live is not mentioned in the biblical text. Tradition, however, identifies the town as *En Keren* (written variously as *Ein Karem* or *En Karim*), some five miles south of Jerusalem (Pax 1970, 58). *Beth-haccherem* may be the location of *En Keren* (Monson 1979, map 12-3). With tradition only as our guide, we will never be able to know with certainty where Zacharias and Elizabeth lived.

[20] (p 6) Luke 1:42-45. Either Elizabeth, prior to Mary's arrival, is supernaturally informed about Mary's angelic encounter and subsequent pregnancy (perhaps just like Mary is informed by Gabriel about Eliza-

beth's pregnancy), or the Holy Spirit is at this very moment supernaturally revealing to Elizabeth everything that had happened to Mary back in Nazareth. In one way or another, Elizabeth knows everything about Mary's conversation with and response to Gabriel recorded in Luke 1:28-38. This knowledge of Mary's pregnancy and of Mary's submission to the Word of God gives Elizabeth a context for interpreting the behavior of the child in her womb and for saying what she says to Mary when Mary shows up at Elizabeth and Zacharias' house.

This passage likewise strongly supports the personhood of the fetus. The text would lead us to believe that John the Baptist as a fetus rejoiced and reacted dramatically at the arrival of and upon entering into the presence of Jesus, the fetus, the Messiah.

[21] (p 6) Luke 1:46-55.

[22] (p 8) The biblical text does not specify what prayer request is being answered. In light of Zacharias' later prophecy in Luke 1:67-79 (particularly verse 68), the request might be the historical national prayer for the redemption of Israel. Or, that statement might be referring to God's response to Zacharias and Elizabeth's repeated requests over the years for a child. Contextually the latter seems most likely.

[23] (p 8) It appears that we should understand on the basis of Luke 1:62 that Zacharias is not only mute but is apparently a deaf mute. It could be that the people at the circumcision and naming ceremony do not really know Zacharias and therefore, with their limited contact with Zacharias *assume* that because Zacharias cannot talk he cannot hear. This would explain why *"they made signs to his* [John's] *father, as to what he wanted him called,"* instead of just asking him.

It seems much more likely, however, that those with him and Elizabeth at the naming ceremony are friends who would have had considerable contact with Zacharias over the previous nine months. It might have been that at the outset of Zacharias' loss of speech, some stereotypically assume that if Zacharias cannot speak then obviously he cannot hear. However, it seems reasonable to conclude that if Zacharias can hear but just not speak, relatives and friends would have figured that out rather quickly. The fact, however, that at the naming ceremony, more than nine months after Gabriel took away Zacharias's ability to speak, relatives and friends are making signs trying to get Zacharias to understand their question or request, leads me to believe that Zacharias is not just unable to speak (which is the only limitation mentioned in Luke 1:20) but also unable to hear.

[24] (p 8) Luke 1:18-23. Later in this chapter we learn that technically, Zacharias does not regain his speech until the eighth day after his son's birth, the day that his son is both circumcised and given his name, John (Lk 1:57-64).

[25] (p 8) Luke 1:56.

[26] (p 8) In many cultures of the world, it is the responsibility of the older women to prepare younger women for marriage and childbirth.

[27] (p 8) Luke 1:6.

[28] (p 8) According to Acts 20:36-38, farewell hugs and kisses are apparently common practice.

CHAPTER 3

[29] (p 9) Bethlehem is some 80 miles south of Nazareth. Given Mary's condition and the mountainous terrain, Mary and Joseph probably do not travel more than 10-12 miles a day. To travel that far each day, they would have to average about two miles an hour (a slow walk) for five to six hours a day. They well could have traveled faster than that and made it in less than a week.

[30] (p 9) Luke 1:56.

[31] (p 9) Nowhere does the biblical text indicate that Mary takes the initiative to either inform or explain to Joseph (or her parents) about her supernatural pregnancy (neither before Mary leaves for Judea nor after

she returns). Matthew simply says, "... *before they came together she <u>was found to be with child</u> by the Holy Spirit*" (Mt 1:18, emphasis added). This phrase suggests that Joseph does not know of Mary's pregnancy until she returns from Judea almost four months pregnant. (See endnote 3, pp 62- 63.) It could be, however, that Mary tries to explain it all but Joseph refuses to believe her.

[32] (p 9) Again, the biblical text is perplexing since one would assume that somewhere along the way Mary must have tried to explain to Joseph her side of the story, including Gabriel's visit and the Holy Spirit coming upon her.

One might argue that perhaps the culture of that day keeps Mary from defending herself. However, it does not seem likely that the culture silences Mary simply because she is a woman, or prohibits her from defending herself. The Mosaic Law consistently affirms the rights of women (though culturally different than in a 21st century, Western democracy), and provides a process for gathering facts in the search for truth.

One would also think that the accuracy of Mary's story about Elizabeth and Zacharias' pregnancy should have counted as some kind of *believability collateral* with respect to the *angel story* and the Holy Spirit-conception-story. Surely a righteous man like Joseph would be looking for some sort of reason to believe his wife. The biblical text, however, does not give even the slightest indication either that the two of them discuss the pregnancy in general or that Mary tries to explain her pregnancy in particular. The silence is deafening.

Equally perplexing is the fact that if Mary does tell her side of the story and Joseph does not believe her, Joseph in essence is calling Mary a liar. He would essentially be saying, "I don't trust you and I don't believe you"—harsh words from a man who is said to be righteous and is shown to be so gracious. Also, in Matthew 1:20, when the angel appears to Joseph in a dream, the angel does not say, "*What Mary told you about her pregnancy is true ....*" Instead, the angel straightforwardly says, "*... do not be afraid to take Mary as your wife, for that which has been conceived in her is of the Holy Spirit.*"

These textual inclusions and exclusions lead us to conclude that perhaps Mary did not, in fact, try to defend herself in any way or give her side of the story at all, hard as that is to believe. We must content ourselves with what the text says, condensed and limited though that may actually be, regarding how, and when, and by whom it is discovered Mary is pregnant. The text merely states, "... *before they came together she was found to be with Child of the Holy Spirit*" (Mt 1:18).

[33] (p 9) Matthew 1:19.

[34] (p 11) Matthew 1:18-24. While the biblical text identifies the angel who appears to both Zacharias and Mary as Gabriel, the Scriptures do not give the reader the name of the angels that repeatedly appear to Joseph in dreams. In Matthew 1, the text says concerning Joseph, "*an angel of the Lord appeared to him in a dream*" (Mt 1:20). The angel is probably Gabriel, but we do not know for sure. In Luke 1, the angel who appears to Zacharias is at first only referred to as "*an angel of the Lord*" (Lk 1:11). The angel later identifies himself as Gabriel (Lk 1:19). And the author, Luke, reveals to his readers that the angel who appears to Mary is Gabriel (Lk 1:26), though the text never indicates that the angel identified himself to Mary as Gabriel.

[35] (p 11) "*And Joseph arose from his sleep, and did as the angel of the Lord commanded him, and took her as his wife*" (Mt 1:24). From this verse it appears that the very next day after Joseph's dream, Joseph formally and publicly finalizes the second stage of marriage by bringing Mary to his house and starting to live with her (cf. Mt 2:13-14). The biblical text does not mention a celebration normally held in connection with this milestone event.

[36] (p 11) Sexual relations between *betrothed* persons, though not the cultural norm, may not have been considered *sinful* because of the binding nature of the initial marriage covenant. McHugh notes, however, "It was only in Judaea, and even there only after A.D. 135, that consummation of the union during the period of betrothal was regarded as normal .... Even after A.D. 135 the Galileans regarded intimate relations before marriage as unseemly or wrong ..." (McHugh 1975, 162-63).

Nowhere in the biblical text does Joseph publicly deny his involvement in Mary's pregnancy. Neither do we find Mary or Joseph explaining to others the baby's supernatural conception. It may be that as far as the people of Nazareth (and perhaps even Mary's and Joseph's families) know, Joseph is the child's father (Keener 1997, 63). Joseph takes Mary to live with him to give legitimacy to the pregnancy. Throughout the New Testament, Joseph is often straightforwardly declared to be Jesus' father.

Luke states that when Jesus begins His ministry, He is *"about thirty years of age, being supposedly the son of Joseph ..."* (Lk 3:23). When Jesus ministers in Nazareth and speaks eloquently in the synagogue, the people are amazed by His speech, commenting, *"Is this not Joseph's son?"* (Lk 4:22). Matthew's account of this event records the people's response to Jesus like this: *"Is not this the carpenter's son? Is not His mother called Mary, and His brothers, James and Joseph and Simon and Judas? And His sisters, are they not all with us? Where then did this man get all these things?"* (Mt 13:55-56). And later on in Jesus' ministry, the Jews, in response to Jesus' claim that He came down out of heaven, observe, *"Is not this Jesus, the son of Joseph, whose father and mother we know?"* (Jn 6:22).

Rumors about Jesus' conception, however, may also follow Him into adulthood. John 8:41 states, *"They [the Jews] said to Him, 'We were not born of fornication* [leaving unsaid perhaps the implication, 'like You were']; *we have one Father, even God.'"* And later in that chapter, *"The Jews answered and said to Him, 'Do we not say rightly that You are a Samaritan and have a demon?'"* (Jn 8:48). Samaritans are *half-breeds*, the result of Jews inter-marrying with re-located, pagan prisoners of war. Relocation is a war strategy used to weaken tribal and territorial identity. The Jews' derogatory statements, therefore, may simply be cultural slurs to discredit Jesus. However they may also point to persistent questions about Mary's pregnancy.

When Mary returns pregnant from her visit to Elizabeth, the word on the street no doubt is that Joseph is the baby's father, even though Joseph and Mary at this point are not yet living together. However, since Mary had to travel through Samaria both going to and returning from Judea, some of the people of Nazareth might well have jumped to the conclusion that Mary has had sexual relations with either a Samaritan or Gentile on that trip, making Jesus a *half-breed*.

Once Joseph brings Mary into his house to live with her, the cultural expectation is that they have sexual relations. However, lest there ever be a doubt about the supernatural nature of the baby's conception, Matthew lets the reader know that Joseph and Mary do not have sexual relations until after the baby is born. Joseph *"kept her a virgin* [lit. 'was not knowing her'] *until she gave birth to a Son"* (Mt 1:25). Matthew's statement implies that Mary and Joseph have sexual relations once the baby is born.

The Israelite culture, like many cultures, relies upon a garment (sheet, piece of cloth) stained with the blood from the wife's hymen (which tears and bleeds the first time a woman has intercourse [Wheat 1977, 51-53]) as evidence of the woman's virginity. This cultural practice is referred to in Deuteronomy 22:13-19 (Keil 1973, 410-11).

Mary's virginity, therefore, could have been proven if, after Mary and Joseph entered into Stage Two of their marriage, they would have had sexual relations and produced a blood-stained garment ... something that would have been impossible to produce after giving birth to a baby. Joseph believes the angel Gabriel and does not insist on the physical evidence of virginity. Keeping Mary a virgin to underscore Jesus' divinity is more important to Joseph than satisfying his curiosity (Keener 1997, 63).

Interestingly, although Joseph begins living with Mary as soon as the angel confirms in a dream the divine origin of her pregnancy (Mt 1:24), Luke describes Mary and Joseph as still *betrothed* [in the first stage of marriage] when they leave for Bethlehem: *"And Joseph also went up from Galilee, from the city of Nazareth, to Judea, to the city of David, which is called Bethlehem, because he was of the house and family of David, in order to register, along with Mary, who was <u>engaged</u>* [betrothed] *to him, and was with child"* (Lk 2:4,5, emphasis added).

Luke's use of the word *betrothed* to describe Mary and Joseph's relationship when they leave for Bethlehem indicates that the concept of *betrothal* primarily describes a marriage relationship that is not yet sexually consummated. Since Matthew lets us in on the bedroom secret that Mary and Joseph, though living together, do not have sexual relations until after the baby is born, Dr. Luke technically and accurately still regards Mary and Joseph as *betrothed* when they travel to Bethlehem.

CHAPTER 4

[37] (p 13) Luke 2:1-3. The biblical text gives no indication as to when exactly the decree is announced. I insert the declaration of the decree at this point into the story because it seems to fit the flow of the narrative, and because in the biblical text the edict is mentioned right on the heels of Mary visiting Elizabeth.

[38] (p 13) "In the Roman Empire periodical censuses were taken with the double object of assessing taxation and of discovering those who were liable for compulsory military service. The Jews were exempt from military service, and, therefore, in Palestine a census would be predominantly for taxation purposes. Regarding these censuses, we have definite information as to what happened in Egypt and almost certainly what happened in Egypt happened in Syria, too, and Judaea was part of the province of Syria …Such censuses were taken every fourteen years. From A.D. 20 until about A.D. 270, we possess actual documents from every census taken. If the fourteen-year cycle held good in Syria, this census must have been in 8 B.C. and that was the year in which Jesus was born" (Barclay 1975, 20).

Hoehner, however, notes that while all of the Roman Empire is from time to time subject to a census, the entire Roman Empire is never required to register simultaneously. Different provinces mandate censuses at different times (Hoehner 1977, 15).

It seems most logical that the fastest mode of communication was on horseback. Historically, this was the means of rapid dissemination of important information in rather vast empires. The use of couriers was common, for example, in Assyria at the time of Esther and Mordecai (Est 3:11-15; 8:13-14).

[39] (p 13) Although Roman law allows property owners to register their land anywhere within a province, some provinces require registration in one's home town (Hoehner 1977, 15).

[40] (p 13) (1) Because of limited historical documents, (2) because of an apparent conflict with Josephus' history, (3) because Quirinus was twice governor of Syria (about a decade apart), and (4) because of several possible meanings of some of the Greek words in the biblical text, dating this census in relation to Quirinius, governor of Syria (Lk 2:2) is one of the most difficult chronological challenges of the New Testament (Hoehner 1977, 16-23). According to Harrison, "The decree was issued about 8 B.C., but probably did not actually go into effect until a few years later" (Harrison, Pfieffer 1962, 1032). Hoehner's extensive discussion of this topic concludes that the census "was probably taken sometime between 6 and 4 B.C." (Hoehner 1977, 23). The taxation process probably takes about 14 years to complete (Harrison 1962, 194). It appears, therefore, that given the communication, travel, and cultural realities of that day, Mary and Joseph were probably not pressured by an urgent census deadline.

[41] (p 13) The biblical text is unclear as to what *specifically* triggers the exact timing of Mary and Joseph's trip to Bethlehem. Caesar Augustus' decree is clearly the overarching reason why Mary and Joseph go to Bethlehem (Lk 2:1-5). Luke 2:3, however, does not so much indicate *urgency* (as we so often read into that verse) as it does *necessity*. All Luke is saying in 2:3 is that people need to comply and are complying: "*And all were proceeding to register for the census, every one to his own city.*"

It seems reasonable to conclude, therefore, that because of distance and travel issues as well as resistance in some provinces, rigid deadlines are not strictly enforced. The urgency for the trip to Bethlehem, therefore, is not so much created by a census deadline as it is by the discovery of Mary's pregnancy. Morris states, "We should perhaps reflect that it was the combination of a decree by the emperor in distant Rome and the gossiping tongues of Nazareth that brought Mary to Bethlehem at just the (sic.) time to fulfill the prophecy about the birthplace of the Christ (Mi 5:2)" (Morris 1974, 84). What Satan means for evil, God can use for good (Gen 50:20).

⁴² (p 15) Mary could well be only five to seven months pregnant when she and Joseph leave Nazareth for Bethlehem. It is doubtful that they would have delayed much longer. The trip to Bethlehem is apparently not perceived to be unusually risky for a woman that far along in her pregnancy. In many cultures of the world, it is not unusual for pregnant women to work and do considerable walking right up to the time of delivery.

The King James translation, *"to be registered with Mary, his espoused wife, being great with child"* (Lk 2:5, emphasis added) technically does not help us in this regard. The Greek word *enkuos*, which Luke uses in Luke 2:5 to describe Mary's condition, simply means *with child* or *pregnant*. The King James Version's use of the word *"great"* no doubt has contributed to the notion over the years that Mary was on the verge of having her baby when they arrived in Bethlehem.

In hindsight, we know that Jesus had to be born in Bethlehem as prophesied in the Old Testament. Jesus ends up being born in Bethlehem, however, because of a series of natural, yet providentially arranged, events and choices.

⁴³ (p 15) Since hospitality in general and staying with relatives in particular are first century cultural norms in the Middle East (just as they are in many parts of the world today), it is reasonable to conclude that Mary and Joseph plan to stay with relatives once they get to Bethlehem. Being of *"the house and family of David"* (Lk 2:4), Joseph undoubtedly has relatives living in David's historical village of Bethlehem. Just as Mary knows Elizabeth, her relative, in a village not far from Bethlehem (who would have provided lodging for Mary and Joseph and have helped with the delivery if there had absolutely been no place to stay in

Bethlehem), it is reasonable to conclude that Joseph knows his extended family in Bethlehem. It is hard to imagine that Joseph and Mary's parents feel good about sending Mary to Bethlehem to give birth to her first child if they do not have the assurance that Mary will be well attended to by family in Bethlehem.

The fact that the traditional Christmas story replaces this Middle Eastern commitment to family and hospitality with Western individualism and isolationism illustrates how far the Christmas tradition has strayed from reality. Though the text does not explicitly mention the involvement of relatives, their involvement would be assumed by first century readers. Jesus' birth in the home of a relative fits harmoniously with both the culture and the text as the story unfolds. [See endnote 54, pp 81-87.]

CHAPTER 5

[44] (p 17) No donkey is mentioned in the biblical text. It is very possible, however, that a donkey or two are used to carry provisions for the trip and food supplies for Mary and Joseph's host family in Bethlehem. It is common in many parts of the world today to take food along for the relatives one is planning to stay with for a period of time.

While it was not uncommon for women to ride saddled donkeys (e.g., Abigail in 1 Sam 25:20, 42 and Moses' wife and children, Ex 4:20), the text does not mention Mary riding one. In fact, "... it was normal for a man to ride and a woman to walk .... If Mary rode the donkey and Joseph walked alongside, which is traditional in Christian art, then Joseph would have been the laughingstock of fellow travelers" (Gower 1987, 240). Being five months or more pregnant, it may also have been safer and more comfortable to walk than to ride.

[45] (p 17) The maps on pages 18 and 53 are based upon the EAST-oriented maps in the *Student Map Manual: Historical Geography of the Bible Lands* (Monson 1979), developed for and used by Jerusalem University

College (JUC; formerly known as the Institute of Holy Land Studies). The following rationale for their EAST-oriented map of Palestine is given in the introduction to the *Student Map Manual*, produced by Pictorial Archive.

"All Pictorial Archive mapping is EAST-oriented. This is not as heretical as it might at first appear. The Bible itself is East-oriented too, as the Hebrew words for the points of the compass indicate (Viz. *Yamin, Semol, Qedem, Ahor & Yam*: see Genesis 13.14; Isaiah 9.11; and Psalm 89.13, etc.). The Medeba Mosaic map is one of the most ancient available and it is East-oriented, as are many other early Mediaeval maps. However, the main reason for the RETURN to East-orientation was dictated by the WIDE SCREEN PROJECT in which the wide screen format necessitated a HORIZONTAL map for inclusion in the audio-visual presentations. Since the map of the Holy Land is elongated along its North-South axis, there was no alternative but to turn the map and East-orientation was chosen, rather than West-orientation, because of the Biblical precedent. However, this new orientation to the East conferred other important advantages, which might have justified this change on their own" (Monson 1979, 2).

The EAST-oriented map of the Holy Land likewise fits the horizontal format of this book. However, more importantly, this unique geographical orientation helps all of us who have a 21st century, Western mindset to look at biblical geography through the cultural lens of its time. It helps us more clearly see and more closely re-create Mary and Joseph's *"Global Positioning System"* as they look at and think about their world.

[46] (p 17) Heading south from Nazareth, there are three primary routes travelers can choose as they cross the Jezreel Valley. Travelers can bear left (east) and travel through the Harod and Beth-shan Valleys to connect with the north-south Jordan Valley. Travelers can bear right (west) and head for either the Megiddo Pass or the Jokneam Pass which would take them through the Mountains of Carmel and then south down the coastal plain of the Mediterranean Sea. Or, travelers can continue straight toward Jerusalem via Ginae and

Samaria. When Jesus makes His last trip from Galilee to Jerusalem, He and His disciples travel down the Jordan Valley to Jericho, then proceed up to Jerusalem through the Judean wilderness. The wise men no doubt traveled down at least part of the Jordan Valley and then up to Jerusalem through the Judean wilderness. [See endnote 102, pp 101.]

[47] (p 17) The journey from Jericho (elevation: 1,018 ft. below sea level) to Jerusalem (elevation: 2,618 ft. above sea level) involves a 12-mile, 3,600 foot climb through the hot Judean wilderness. The road is notoriously dangerous, as reflected in Jesus' parable of the Good Samaritan (Lk 10:30-37).

[48] (p 17) At times, Jesus goes through Samaria when traveling between Galilee and Jerusalem. In John 4, Jesus stops in Sychar and meets the Samaritan woman at the well. On another occasion when Jesus is traveling toward Jerusalem, He sends His disciples out ahead to make arrangements for Him. The Samaritan village, however, does not receive Him, so they go on to another village (Lk 9:51-56).

[49] (p 19) Luke 2:4 states that Mary and Joseph *"went **up** from Galilee, from the city of Nazareth, to Judea, to the city of David, which is called Bethlehem ..."* (emphasis added). Because Jerusalem (elevation: 2,618 ft.) and Bethlehem (elevation: 2,250 ft.) are located at some of the highest elevations in the hills of Judea, travelers from virtually everywhere in Palestine must geographically go up to get there. The exception would be if one approaches Bethlehem and Jerusalem from Hebron (elevation 3,000 ft.) to the south. Even then, the last part of the undulating road geographically takes one up into Jerusalem. Years later, Jesus *"went down"* from Jerusalem to Nazareth with His parents (Lk 2:51).

In North American culture, our point of reference is north. We describe things as they would appear on a map, not topographically. From Omaha, Nebraska, we would say we are going *up* to Minneapolis, Minnesota and *down* to Wichita, Kansas.

Mary and Joseph's route no doubt takes them through Genae, up past beautiful Samaria (former capital of the ten northern tribes of Israel and re-built by Herod the Great), past Shechem, then along the ridge road to Jerusalem.

[50] (p 19) This common, historical practice is described by W. M. Christie in his discussion of the "Earliest Night Resting-Places" and charts the development of roadside inns (Christie 1960, 1470).

[51] (p 19) Bethlehem is just five miles south of Jerusalem. *Beth-lehem* (literally meaning "house of Bread" in Hebrew), located in Judah, was probably so named because of its production of grain (cf. the Book of Ruth).

[52] (p 19) There is no suggestion in the biblical text that Mary and Joseph arrive at night. While Bethlehem is close to Jerusalem, Mary and Joseph probably timed their arrival so as to arrive during the day. Arriving after dark creates more drama for the traditional Christmas pageant, but is probably a reflection of Western culture where travelers pull into a motel after dark. The wise men, on the other hand, following the star that reappeared, probably arrive at dusk.

CHAPTER 6

[53] (p 21) Bethlehem is nestled on a hillside on the road from Jerusalem to Hebron. The road from Jerusalem (elevation: 2,618 ft.) to Hebron (elevation: 3,000 ft.) undulates through the Judean hills, ultimately rising some 400 feet. The road from Jerusalem to Bethlehem (elevation: 2,250 ft.), however, drops almost 400 feet. Travelers from the north, therefore, descend into Bethlehem.

[54] (p 21) Most Christians have never even thought about (let alone seriously considered) the possibility that Joseph and Mary stay in the home of relatives once they get to Bethlehem. There are at least eight reasons why the traditional story developed the way it did.

(1) The first and most obvious reason why Christians have historically believed the local inn was the only lodging option available to Mary and Joseph in Bethlehem is because the English Bible translators translated the Greek word "kataluma" as "inn." Why we think of an inn and a stable when we read Luke 2:7 and not a private home is because of the way the translators chose to translate the Greek text.

The Greek word *kataluma* (translated "inn" in Luke 2:7), can be, and elsewhere in the New Testament is translated "guest room" an extra room in a private home to accommodate guests (Mk 14:13-15; Lk 22:8-12). This means that if the translation "guest room" would have been used in the English text of Luke 2:7, then those reading the biblical account would have concluded that Joseph and Mary's plan was to find lodging in the guest room of a private home (probably that of a relative). When the baby is born, however, Mary and Joseph are not in the privacy of a guest room as one would have expected, and the text tells us why. It is because the guest room is occupied.

For Joseph and Mary to first check out the possibility of staying with *relatives* also makes good sense economically since Mary and Joseph appear to be of humble means. At least later, Joseph and Mary apparently do not have the resources to offer a lamb for a burnt offering when dedicating Jesus at the Temple. Instead, they substitute a turtledove for the burnt offering (Lk 2:22-24) as allowed by the Law of Moses for those who cannot afford a lamb (Lev 12:8). Given their financial condition, staying with relatives is Joseph and Mary's cheapest and most reasonable option—especially if they had anticipated staying in Bethlehem for any length of time.

(2) The second reason the Christmas story traditionally pictures Jesus as born in an isolated stable instead of in the home of relatives is because even though Matthew unambiguously states in his Nativity narrative, "... *and they* [the wise men] *came into the house and saw the Child with Mary His mother* ..." (Mt 2:11, emphasis added), it is assumed that this reference to a house does not fit. Baby Jesus, after all, is placed in a feed trough

(Lk 2:7). This presumably means that when the wise men find Jesus and worship Him in a house (Mt 2:11), Matthew must be describing an event that takes place sometime after Jesus' birth.

Bible interpreters *resolve* this dilemma and seeming contradiction by creating a two-year gap between the birth of Jesus *in a stable* and the arrival of the wise men to worship Jesus *in a house*. Possible? Yes. Probable and logical? In my opinion, no. In fact, to arrive at such a conclusion one must align one's self with Herod's interpretation of the wise men's story. And aligning oneself with the mechanizations of Herod's paranoid mind (see endnote 101, pp 98-101) seems less than wise! What Herod concludes, of course, is that the star first appears to the wise men the night the King of the Jews is born. It then takes the wise men two years to decide that the star is connected to the birth of a Jewish king and that they should travel to Jerusalem.

Why Mary and Joseph would still be in Bethlehem two years later, of course, is anybody's guess. The biblical text gives no hint whatsoever that Joseph and Mary are anticipating a long stay or permanent move when they leave Nazareth. Staying for several months (given the pregnancy) is one thing. Two years is very different. If Mary and Joseph do stick around Bethlehem for two years, they are by this time a burden to relatives, leaning pretty hard on new friends they have made, or at some point have bought themselves a house. When we put to the *sniff test* all these factors and explanations as to why Mary and Joseph are residing in a house when the wise men supposedly show up in Bethlehem two years later, things smell a little fishy.

Of course, even if the star appears some two years before the wise men arrive does not mean that the star first appears the night Jesus is born. Clearly, God could have caused the star to appear two years *before* Jesus' birth so that after all their deliberations, plans and travel the wise men would arrive in Bethlehem *at* the time of Jesus' birth in just as timely a manner as did Joseph and Mary.

(3) The third reason why Christians picture Mary and Joseph in an isolated stable instead of in the home of a relative is because according to Luke 2:7, Jesus is laid in a manger (i.e., feed trough), and mangers, it is assumed, are only found in stables. What such logic fails to take into account culturally, however, is that

house-barns were common in that part of the world. (See endnote 57, pp 88-90). In that setting, Jesus could have been born in a house yet placed in a manger.

The solution, therefore, to the apparent conflict between the word *feed trough* in Luke 2:7 and the word *house* in Matthew 2:11 is found in the fact that Luke does not actually say that Mary and Joseph are in a stable. He only says that after the baby is born he is placed in a feed trough, which, it is assumed, places Mary and Joseph in a stable. The idea of an isolated stable, therefore, is solely based upon a single thread of circumstantial evidence—namely the one word, *"manger,"* found in Luke 2:7.

(4) A fourth reason Christians prefer thinking of Jesus being born in a isolated stable rather than on the home of relatives is because they either are ignorant of or fail to factor in, the cultural reality that in many parts of the world hosting relatives and friends, even strangers, has been and continues to be a cultural expectation. In fact, the compound Greek word for "hospitality," *philoxenia*, literally means *"love of the stranger."* The Latin American value embedded in the phrase, *nuestra casa es su casa* ("our house is your house") is taken to an even higher level in Middle Eastern culture where hospitality is one of its most highly valued virtues. For Joseph and Mary to arrive in Joseph's family's *hometown*, (being of *"the house and lineage of David"* Lk 2:4) and not have a place to stay is, in my opinion, culturally unthinkable. Having lived a good number of years in Latin America, having visited more than 30 countries, and having been exposed to the high value the Middle East places on hospitality through my studies in and numerous visits to that part of the world, I find the isolated stable scenario sociologically disjointed and culturally suspect. Not only does such a theory go contrary to culture, it makes Mary and Joseph and their families appear shortsighted, incompetent, and rather foolish for not thinking through the implications of sending pregnant Mary and Joseph off to Bethlehem by themselves to have their first child.

(5) The fifth reason why the traditional Christmas story pictures Mary and Joseph all by themselves in a stable instead of in the company of family and friends is because the "isolation image" is so much a part of

the traditional story that when Luke 2:16-19 is read the reader's eyes are blind to and the hearer's ears are deaf to the clear reference to others being with Mary and Joseph when the shepherds tell their story. (See endnote 69, pp 93-94.)

(6 and 7) The sixth and seventh reasons why Christians resist the idea that Joseph and Mary stay with relatives in Bethlehem are (6) because the text does not explicitly say so, and (7) because it is assumed that if relatives would have been involved, the biblical writers would surly have mentioned it. My response to those objections would simply be that all history is selective history and all historians omit details for three principal reasons.

First, historians omit details because of their *literary purpose*. Writers selectively include and exclude details in keeping with their central theme and ultimate goal. Certain details, though interesting, are not really germane to the writer's purpose. Secondly, historians omit details because of their *worldview*. Middle Eastern, holistic thinking is much more focused on the big picture than it is on the specificity of details with which the dichotomizing Western mind is preoccupied. And thirdly, historians omit details because of their *cultural frame of reference*. Historians (including the biblical writers) assume that the readers understand the cultural context of the story and therefore do not feel compelled to include certain details.

The following examples of strategic omissions by the Gospel writers indicate that they often omit interesting, even important, details that they could have (and from our stand point perhaps should have) included in the biblical text.
- Only Matthew mentions that Joseph marries [lit. "took"] Mary after Gabriel appears to him.
- Only Luke mentions Joseph and Mary's trip to Bethlehem and the actual birth of Jesus.
- Luke makes it clear that other people are present when the shepherds tell their story, but like Matthew, Luke gives no clue as to who these people are or why they are there.

- Matthew records the visit of the wise men but neither says how many of them there are nor from where specifically they come. Matthew also says nothing about when in relation to Jesus' birth the star appears.
- Matthew tells us that Joseph and Mary are in a house when the wise men arrive in Bethlehem, though he does not say in the house of whom.
- Luke completely omits the *detail* that Joseph and Mary and Baby Jesus flee to Egypt
- All four gospels record the feeding of the 5,000. Three out of the four, however, make no mention of the young boy who brought the five barley loaves and two fishes. Only John includes that strategic detail (Jn 6:9)!
- All four gospels include the story of Jesus coming to the disciples walking on the water. Only Matthew, however, mentions Peter's amazing walk on water (Mt 14:28)! How could the other writers possibly omit this dramatic part of the story?
- All four gospel writers mention that one of Jesus' disciples cuts off the high priest's servant's ear at the time of Jesus' arrest. Only John, however, identifies the sword-wielding disciple as Peter and the high priest's servant as Malchus (Jn 18:10). Luke and John note it is the servant's *right* ear. Only Dr. Luke (Col 4:14) mentions that Jesus miraculously reattaches the ear.
- Peter is evidently married ... at least Jesus heals Peter's mother-in-law (Lk 4:38) and Paul asks, "*Do we not have a right to take along a believing wife, even as the rest of the apostles, and the brothers of the Lord and Cephas?*" (1 Cor 9:5). Yet no wife of any of the Twelve Apostles is so identified in the biblical record.
- And, Joseph apparently dies before Jesus does (to us a rather significant detail), though nowhere in the Gospels is Joseph's death mentioned. That Mary is widowed seems apparent when from the cross Jesus asks John to care for Mary (Jn 19:26-27).

All history, therefore, is selective history, with authors often omitting culturally assumed details. So, just because Joseph's relatives in Bethlehem are not mentioned in the biblical text does not mean that Joseph and Mary did not stay with them.

(8) The eighth and final reason why Christians find it difficult if not impossible to accept the idea that Mary gave birth in the home of a relative and not in an isolated stable is because accepting such an idea would wreak havoc with our Christmas carols and our preaching. Take, for example, the *because-there-was-no-room-for-them-in-the-inn* application paradigm of Luke 2:7. The *no-room-for-Jesus* idea *preaches* and the Christmas carol *No Room* is beautiful and penetrating (in fact it is one of my favorites). However, even though at one level evangelical believers are committed to the premise that relevant application must always be based on and grow out of accurate interpretation, change related to biblical interpretation (especially with respect to something as familiar as the Christmas story) on the surface always feels heretical.

Therefore, (1) because Matthew states that Mary and Joseph are in a house, (2) because Luke tells us there are other people present when the shepherds tell their story, (3) because it seems a bit strange to have Mary and Joseph moving to a house and to also still be in Bethlehem two years later, (4) because the Greek word *kataluma* is legitimately translated "*guest room*," (5) because the existence of *house-barns* in the Middle East allows for Jesus to have been born in a house yet laid in a manger, (6) because the cultural expectation would have been for Joseph and Mary to stay with relatives in Bethlehem, and (7) because historians regularly omit details we might think important, it seems to me very probable that Joseph and Mary stayed with relatives during their time in Bethlehem, even though the text does not explicitly say so.

[55] (p 23) Guest rooms are referred to numerous times in Scripture. When Abraham's servant arrived back in Mesopotamia to find a wife for Isaac, the servant asked Rebekah if there was room for him to lodge in her father's house. Rebekah replied, "*We have plenty of both straw and feed, and room to lodge in*" (the latter phrase is translated in the Septuigient, "*a place for you to lodge*" [from the same root as *kataluma*] Gen 24:23-

25, emphasis added). Elijah stays in the guest room (i.e., "upper room") of the widow of Zarephath (1 Ki 17:17-23). The Shunammite woman and her husband build a guest room on the flat roof of their home for the prophet Elisha (2 Ki 4:8-10). Near the end of Jesus' life, Jesus sends Peter and John on a mission, saying, *"Go and prepare the Passover for us, that we may eat it."* They reply, *"Where do You want us to prepare it?"* Jesus responds, *"Behold, when you have entered the city, a man will meet you carrying a pitcher of water; follow him into the house that he enters. And you shall say to the owner of the house, 'The Teacher says to you, "Where is the guest room (kataluma) in which I may eat the Passover with My disciples?"' And he will show you a large, furnished, upper room"* (Lk 22:8-12). Mark also uses the word *kataluma* when recording this event (Mk 14:13-15).

Stephan Pfann (head of the Jerusalem-based Center for the Study of Early Christianity) notes that although *kataluma* can mean inn, guest room, or large room, "The natural thing would have been that they [Mary and Joseph] would be in the guest room" (Laub 1994, 2).

[56] (p 23) The lack of privacy in a one-room dwelling is discussed by Bailey (Bailey 2007, 102).

[57] (p 23) This is Heather Marx's three-dimensional, cut-away rendering of Bailey's one-dimensional sketch of a house-barn (Bailey 1980, 206). Kenneth E. Bailey (Professor of New Testament, Director of the Institute for Middle Eastern New Testament Studies, Near East School of Theology, Beirut, Lebanon) cites scholarly support for translating *kataluma* as *guest room* in Luke 2:7 (Bailey 1980, 214-15). Bailey contends that archaeological research and the Old and New Testament texts confirm the common use of the kind of home described in this Christmas narrative.

Bailey states, "it is necessary to observe the construction of Palestinian traditional one-room homes. Such buildings are split-level homes. There is a small, lower level for the animals at one end. About 80 percent of the one room is a raised terrace on which the family cooks, eats, and lives.

"The two levels are connected by a short set of stairs.

"The reader needs to know that the animals move daily in and out of the house. Thus, in the New Testament and in the Old Testament, there is clear evidence of the existence of the one-room, split-level home such as we suggest for Luke 2:7. Such one-room homes often had/have guest rooms attached to the end or built on the roof for guests.

"In such traditional homes, mangers are built into the floor of the raised terrace on which the family lives. If the cow or donkey is hungry in the night it can stand and reach the feed on the floor of the upper family living space, often about four feet higher than the level for the animals" (Bailey 2003, 4-7).

Bailey notes that Gustaf Dalmann "has nearly a hundred pages of photographs and scale drawings of a wide variety of such peasant homes, all of which fit his two level description ..." (Bailey 1980, 208). Bailey also quotes William Thomson, Presbyterian missionary in Lebanon, Syria, and Palestine for many years, who wrote in 1858, "It is my impression that the birth actually took place in an ordinary house of some common peasant, and that the baby was laid in one of the mangers, such as are still found in the dwellings of farmers in this region" (Thomson 1858, 503). So compelling are the translational, archaeological and cultural considerations behind this new paradigm that the Creation Museum near Cincinnati has replaced the traditional stable in their annual, live nativity with a "more historically accurate" house-barn like the one described in this chapter (*answersupdate* 2010, 3).

Murphy-O'Connor, a senior researcher at Jerusalem's *Ecole Biblique* where Dead Sea Scroll studies were based, states, "The Greek underlying the phrase, *'she laid him in a manger because there was no room for them in the inn'* (Luke 2:7) can also be rendered, *'she laid him in a manger because they had no space in the room.'* We should envisage an overflowing one-room house" (Murphy-O'Connor 1998, 199).

Morris writes, "But it is also possible that the birth took place in a very poor home where the animals share the same roof as the family.... Another possibility is that the word does not mean *inn* here, but a room in a house (as in [Luke] 22:11)" (Morris 1974, 83-84).

The split-level, house-stable architectural design of Middle Eastern homes fits well with the story of Jephthah in Judges 11:30-40. In this passage, Jephthah vows to offer up as a burnt offering "*whatever comes out of the doors of my house to meet me when I return in peace from the sons of Ammon.*" Jephthah's vow is based on the cultural reality that animals routinely wander in and out of the split-level, house-stable homes. He clearly anticipates that one of his significant animals (e.g., goat, sheep, ox) would exit from the stable area of his house (Bailey 2003, 6).

[58] (p 23) This house-stable arrangement appears to be the cultural backdrop of Luke 13:15 (Bailey 1980, 206-07).

[59] (p 23) The biblical text indicates that a period of time elapses between Mary and Joseph's arrival in Bethlehem and when Jesus is born. The text says, "*And it came about that <u>while they were there, the days were completed</u> for her to give birth*" (Lk 2:6, emphasis added).

It is impossible to know precisely how Mary and Joseph spend their days in Bethlehem since the biblical text does not provide that kind of detail. It is reasonable to assume, however, that the registration and taxation process takes a bit of time and that Mary and Joseph engage in rather routine life activities while in Bethlehem.

CHAPTER 7

[60] (p 25) Hoehner concludes that Jesus' "birth would have had to be no earlier than 5 B.C. and it seems that late 5 B.C. or early 4 B.C. best satisfies all the evidence" (Hoehner 1977, 25).

[61] (p 25) Although the text is silent with respect to the delivery, a midwife no doubt assists. Rachel is assisted by a midwife when she goes into severe labor outside of Bethlehem, gives birth to Benjamin, and then dies (Gen 35:17). A midwife is present for Tamar's difficult birth to twins, Perez and Zerah (Gen 38:28).

Midwives help deliver the Hebrew babies in Egypt (Ex 1:15-22). And when Phinehas' wife goes into labor after receiving word that her husband has been killed in battle, *"the woman who stood by her"* (i.e., the midwife) encourages the dying mother to no avail. Older female relatives often function in this role.

[62] (p 25) The biblical text does not state explicitly what time of the day Jesus was born. The angel, however, who spoke to the shepherds that evening as they kept *"watch over their flocks by night"* (Lk 2:8, emphasis added), told the shepherds, *"today in the city of David there has been born for you, a Savior, who is Christ the Lord"* (Lk 2:11, emphasis added). Since the Jewish day begins at 6:00 p.m., and the angels appear to the shepherds at night, we conclude that Jesus was probably born early evening—after 6:00 p.m. Enough time elapses between the birth and the arrival of the shepherds at the house that evening for things to be cleaned up and for Mary to be ready to receive visitors.

[63] (p 25) This Middle Eastern custom is referred to in Ezekiel 16:4 and is practiced in the Middle East even today (Bailey 1980, 202).

[64] (p 27) In many parts of the world it is not unusual to pronounce a blessing upon a mother and her newborn child. A blessing and prayer of thanksgiving to God are common Jewish practices.

[65] (p 27) No other detail of the Christmas story has more greatly shaped the visual image in the mind of the reader and has more greatly led to embellishments of the narrative than the mention of a manger. There is no mention of a barn, or stable, or corral, or animals, or straw, or manure ... only a manger (feed trough). Put the *manger* and the *inn* together, and presto, out comes the traditional Christmas story complete with an inn, a hard-hearted innkeeper, a stable out back, and a manger filled with straw.

Writing about the first Christmas, Luke states, *"And she wrapped Him in cloths, and laid Him in a manger, because there was no room for them in the inn (kataluma)"* (Lk 2:7). The Greek word *pandokheion*, however, is most commonly used to refer to a public, commercial inn (Bailey 2003, 5). Jesus uses this word to designate the place where the Good Samaritan takes the wounded traveler in the parable of the Good Samaritan

(Lk 10:34). Luke, therefore, is fully aware of this word but chooses not to use it in Luke 2:7. Instead Luke more precisely uses the word *kataluma*, which most likely is to be understood as the guest room. Bailey notes, "... the Arabic and Syriac versions have never, in 1900 years, translated *kataluma* with the word *inn*" (Bailey 2007, 103). When the biblical text is properly understood, both the public inn and its hard-hearted innkeeper evaporate" (Bailey 1980, 214-15).

While animals in first century Palestine are sometimes kept in corral-type stables or caves, a separate, external stable is not required by the biblical text. By too quickly settling for *the obvious*—that Jesus was born in a stable—the culturally-challenged reader is blinded to another, more plausible option—that Jesus was born in a *split-level*, house-barn, peasant home of one of Joseph's relatives as described above. When the reader understands that a feed trough (manger) can be right there in the terraced floor of a split-level house-barn, the text suddenly makes perfect sense when it states, *"And she gave birth to her first-born son; and she wrapped him in cloths, and laid Him in a manger ..."* (Lk 2:7).

According to Bailey, a proper first century understanding of guest rooms, *split-level* house-barns, peasant homes, and feed troughs in living rooms allows the reader to correctly visualize the setting of Luke 2:7.

Now all the parts of the story fall into place. Luke's text was originally written for a Palestinian reader who starts with the assumptions that mangers are in the living room of one-room homes and that guest rooms are attached to one-room homes and are used for guests.

The author records: "And she gave birth to (sic) firstborn son and wrapped him in swaddling cloths and laid him in a manger."

The reader instinctively asks, "Manger? Oh, they are in the main family room! Why not the guest room?"

The author instinctively anticipates the above question and replies, "Because there was no place for them in the guest room (*kataluma*)."

The reader concludes, "Ah, I see. So the guest room was full. Never mind; the family room is more appropriate anyway" (Bailey 2003, 6).

CHAPTER 8

[66] (p 28) In a relatively small community like Bethlehem with a population of some 2,000-3,000 (Laub 1994, 1), it is reasonable to assume that Joseph's relatives know at least the families of the visiting shepherds.

[67] (p 28) Luke 2:16 says, "*And they came with haste and <u>found their way</u> to Mary and Joseph, and the baby as He lay in a manger*" (emphasis added). The phrase "*found their way*" suggests that the shepherds are not given specific directions by the angels, but rather are required to search out Mary and Joseph by asking questions as to if and where a baby has been born that day in Bethlehem.

[68] (p 28) Bailey observes: "The shepherds are told that the presence of the baby in a manger is a sign for them. Shepherds were near the bottom of the social ladder and indeed, their profession was declared unclean by some of their rabbis. Many places will not welcome them. In many homes they will feel their poverty and be ashamed of their low estate. But no—they will face no humiliation as they visit *this* child for he is laid in a manger. That is, he is born in a simple peasant home with the mangers in the family room. He is one of them" (Bailey 1980, 207).

[69] (p 30) The traditional Christmas story always pictures Mary and Joseph alone in the stable. The shepherds arrive and talk only to Mary and Joseph. I have yet to see a Christmas drama or to read a Christmas story book that put other people in the stable with Mary and Joseph.

The biblical text, however, makes it clear that others are in the room with Mary and Joseph when the shepherds give their report. "*And they* [the shepherds] *came with haste and found their way to Mary and Joseph, and the baby as He lay in the manger. And when they had seen this* [obviously while they are still in the house], *they* *made known the statement which had been told them about this Child. And <u>all who heard it</u> wondered at the things which were told them by the shepherds. But Mary treasured up all these things, pondering them in her heart"* (Lk 2:16-19, emphasis added).

It is sometimes suggested that the shepherds publicly make known their story out on the streets. This distortion makes for a great application regarding evangelism but is not what the text says. This distortion seems to be necessary to perpetuate the myth and emotional drama of Mary and Joseph being all by themselves in an isolated stable. The text, however, clearly communicates that the reciting of the shepherds' story is done inside the house where Mary as well as others (probably Joseph's relatives) hear and emotionally respond to the shepherds' amazing experience. The wording of the text fits nicely with the related interlocking pieces of the Christmas story.

CHAPTER 9

[70] (p 31) Luke 2:10-12. The angel who appears to the shepherds does not explicitly invite or command the shepherds to go (either yet that night or in the days to come) to Bethlehem to celebrate the Messiah's birth and witness this historic event. The angel, however, assumes that the shepherds will go and tells them what they will find and see when they get there.

These Jewish shepherds give no indication that they think it strange that the Messiah would be born. Their understanding of the Messiah coming as an infant is consistent with the understanding of the Jewish leaders in Jerusalem who later are questioned by King Herod as to where the King of the Jews is to be born.

[71] (p 31) Luke 2:13-14.
[72] (p 33) Luke 2:15-16.
[73] (p 33) Luke 2:19.
[74] (p 33) Luke 2:20.

CHAPTER 10

[75] (p 34) Male circumcision is given to Abraham and his descendants as a sign of their covenant with God (Gen 17:1-27) and is to be performed when the male child is eight days old (Gen 17:12). Circumcision is later required by the Law of Moses (Lev 12:1-3). In the New Testament we find that with respect both to Elizabeth and Zacharias' son, John (Lk 1:59-63), and Mary and Joseph's son, Jesus (Lk 2:21), the male child is officially named on the day he is circumcised.

[76] (p 34) Mary (Lk 1:31-33) and Joseph (Mt 1:21) are both told what their baby boy's name is to be: *"And when eight days were completed before His circumcision, His name was then called Jesus, the name given by the angel before He was conceived in the womb"* (Lk 2:21).

[77] (p 34) Leviticus 12:4-5.

[78] (p 34) Leviticus 12:6-7.

[79] (p 36) Luke 2:22.

[80] (p 36) Leviticus 12:8. Since Luke only refers to turtledoves and young pigeons, making no reference to a lamb (Lk 2:24), it seems reasonable to conclude that Mary and Joseph were too poor to offer a lamb.

[81] (p 36) Luke 2:22-23

[82] (p 36) Numbers 18:14-16

[83] (p 36) Exodus 13:2, 12-13, 15; 22:29. The firstborn males of Israel are apparently redeemed (*purchased*) on an on-going basis throughout their history in two ways. First, the tribe of Levi is given to God, as it were, as a replacement for the firstborn. The tribe of Levi is set apart *by* God and *unto* God for temple service (Num 3:12-13; 8:14-18). Secondly, firstborn males of Israel are redeemed through a special payment to the Levites (Num 18:14-16).

[84] (p 36) Luke 2:22-24 describes a visit to the Temple that merges these two requirements into one.

CHAPER 11

[85] (p 37) Luke 2:25-32 (Contemporary English Version).
[86] (p 37) Luke 2:34-35 (Contemporary English Version).
[87] (p 37) Isaiah 53:1-12; Acts 2:22-24; Acts 4:1-12.
[88] (p 39) Romans 5:1-21.
[89] (p 39) John 1:29, 36; Romans 3:25.
[90] (p 39) Romans 5:8; 1 John 2:2.
[91] (p 39) John 1:11-12; John 3:16.
[92] (p 39) Acts 17:30-31.
[93] (p 39) Luke 2:36-38.
[94] (p 40) For a thorough discussion of this subject, read Gary Smalley and John Trent's insightful book, *The Blessing* (Smalley & Trent 1986).

CHAPTER 12

[95] (p 41) Though the text does not explicitly state that Mary and Joseph are making plans to return to Nazareth, it is reasonable to assume that Mary and Joseph finish their registration and taxation in Bethlehem since they immediately take off for Egypt as soon as Joseph is told by an angel to do so.

[96] (p 41) We face a dilemma of sorts regarding the time of the day the wise men left Jerusalem and arrived in Bethlehem. The fact that the wise men saw the star (Mt 2:10) leads one to believe it was dark, perhaps dusk, because stars come out at night. Since Bethlehem is only five miles south of Jerusalem, the wise men could have left Jerusalem around dusk, getting to Bethlehem at night, but not too late. There would be

some logic and courtesy about staying overnight in Jerusalem so as to not impose on anyone for supper by arriving too late. But if the wise men stay overnight in Jerusalem and take off in the morning, the appearance of the star during the day seems out of place. The appearance of the star would indicate an evening arrival in Bethlehem.

[97] (p 41) Since the biblical text does not specify how many wise men there were, over the centuries Christian art and church writings depict and describe anywhere from two to twelve wise men (Barclay 1975, 31). As centuries pass, however, the Western Church culturally concludes that the three gifts strongly suggest three wise men, who in the 7th century A.D. are given names—Caspar, Melchior and Balthasar. The Eastern Church, meanwhile, in keeping with its own traditions and cultural emphasis upon community, concludes that there are 12 wise men whose gift to Jesus consists of three items—gold, frankincense and myrrh. To highlight our uncertainty about the exact number of wise men, I have increased their number from the traditional three to five.

[98] (p 41) Examples of Middle Eastern hospitality are found in Genesis 18:1-8; 19:1-3; 24:31-33, Judges 19:21 and Luke 11:5-8—the animals are fed, the travelers given water to wash their feet, and a meal is prepared for the guests.

Camels are not mentioned in the Matthew text, though it is very possible that the wise men ride and carry their provisions on camels (see Gen 24:10-14). The wise men undoubtedly travel with servants.

CHAPTER 13

[99] (p 43) The wise men's motivation for their trip is revealed in Matthew 2:1-2. The wise men state that they have come to Jerusalem because of a strange, kingly star (perhaps alluded to in Num 24:17) which

they had seen while in their homeland to the east. The idea is not that the star is to their east, but that they are from the east. If the star is in anyway related geographically to Palestine, the star is in their western sky.

[100] (p 44) According to the biblical text, the *wise men* who visited Jesus were technically *magi*, not kings. The magi (from the Greek, *magos*) belonged to "a sacred caste, originally Median, who apparently conformed to the Persian religion while retaining their old beliefs" (Vine 1996, 679). Though not themselves kings, these men were astrologers who perhaps served the king of Persia (Keeneer 1997, 65), much like the astrologers of Daniel's time who served the kings of Babylon.

The wise men come from the east (Mt 2:1). They may have come from the southeast (Arabia), or the northeast (former Babylon). The fact that Assyria and Babylon take the Jews captive to the northeast perhaps tips the scale toward the wise men coming from the northeast. These astrologers (common in that part of the world) could well have had contact with and have been influenced by the Jews and their Scriptures. We should not rule out the possibility that God directly revealed Himself to them.

[101] (p 44) Matthew 2:1-10. In recent decades, a popular insight into the traditional Christmas story is that the wise men arrive about two years after Jesus' birth. The principal rationale for this conclusion is three-fold.

The first, and perhaps primary, reason why many conclude the wise men arrive about two years after Jesus' birth, is the fact that the text says that the wise men *"came into <u>the house</u>"* (Mt 2:11, emphasis added). The logic goes something like this. Since Jesus is born in a stable, not in a house, yet Mary and Joseph are in a house when the wise men arrive, not in a stable, it follows that quite a period of time must have elapsed between Jesus' birth and the wise men's arrival in Bethlehem.

Hoehner, however, observes, "Furthermore, to say that Jesus was no longer an infant because the Magi visited Him in a house rather than a stable is quite weak. Certainly they would have moved to a house as soon as it was possible. Indeed the tone of Matthew 2:1 is that the Magi visited Christ soon after His birth" (Hoehner 1977, 24).

Secondly, Jesus' birth is deduced to have been two years before the wise men's arrival because of the assumption that the wise men informed King Herod that the star had appeared two years before their arrival in Jerusalem (Mt 2:7,16). The text, however, does not explicitly say that the wise men tell Herod the star appeared two years before. Since Herod *"ascertained from them the time the star appeared"* (Mt 2:7) and then later *"slew all the male children who were in Bethlehem and in all its environs, from two years old and under, according to the time which he had ascertained from the magi"* (Mt 2:16), some conclude (perhaps correctly, perhaps incorrectly) that the wise men tell Herod that the star had appeared two years before. It could be, however, that the wise men say, "about a year and a half ago," with Herod slaughtering all the babies two years old and under to make sure there is no margin for error. Herod, after all, casts his broad, lethal net to "*Bethlehem and all its environs*" [emphasis added] instead of limiting the slaughter to the city of Bethlehem *per se* as communicated to him by the chief priests and scribes (Mt 2:4-6), leaving no margin for error or faulty exegesis. "That Herod killed children up to two years old was only to be sure he got Jesus. This is not out of character with Herod. Therefore, the slaying of the children soon after Christ's birth is tenable" (Hoehner 1977, 24).

We also call into question the logic that concludes the star appeared at the moment of Jesus' birth. Herod concluded that the star appeared at the moment of Jesus' birth (which is why he killed all the boy babies two year old and younger), but Matthew does not make that connection. The star was obviously used by God to get these foreigners in on the birth of Jesus, but the star could well have been sent by God in anticipation of Jesus' birth so that they would arrive in Bethlehem at the time of Jesus' birth.

A third reason some place the arrival of the wise men two years after Jesus' birth is the fact that in Matthew 2:8-23, Matthew refers to Jesus as a *child* (Gk. *paidion*) instead of as an *infant* (Gk. *brephos*) as

Luke does in Luke 2:12. Hoehner, however, points out that the distinction between those two words is not that neat and clean. *Paidion* is used of infants (Lk 1:59, 66, 76; 2:17, 27; Jn 16:21; Heb 11:23) and *brephos* is used by Paul to refer to a young child (2 Tim 3:15) (Hoehner 1977, 24).

Additionally, there are at least four puzzling questions that grow out of a reconstructed Christmas story that has Mary and Joseph homeless when they arrive in Bethlehem and have them still in Bethlehem two years after Jesus' birth. The first has already been alluded to and involves the culturally unthinkable possibility that neither Joseph's relatives, nor residents of Bethlehem, nor Zacharias and Elizabeth, extend hospitality to Joseph and pregnant Mary, forcing them for a time to live in a stable. The second question is somewhat related. If two years later Mary and Joseph are in a house, that means that somebody finally took them in. In which case, how long might Mary and Joseph have had to have stayed in the stable before they overcame their homelessness? A week? A month? Six months? Living for an extended period of time in a stable seems highly untenable. Third, whose house was it and how did they end up there? Did their relatives, though not aware at first, finally find out Joseph and Mary were in town? Or did someone feel sorry for them and take them in? Or, might they have just found a little house to invest in? (It should be noted that all of these possibilities presume or require that Jesus was born almost immediately upon arriving in Bethlehem since a delayed delivery would have gotten Mary and Joseph out of the stable before Jesus was born.) And fourth, why would Mary and Joseph stay in Bethlehem two years? Why did they not return to Nazareth? When they left Nazareth, were they intending to make a permanent move? That Mary and Joseph are still in Bethlehem two years later does not make a whole lot of sense (unless, of course, the tax forms were as complicated to fill out then as they are today!). To me, none of these alternative scenarios are reasonable.

The fact that the star perhaps first appears two years before the wise men arrive in no way requires that the star first appears the night/day Jesus is born. On the contrary, it seems more reasonable that God prepares the wise men ahead of time, orchestrating their arrival at the time of Jesus' birth. This understanding is more consistent with the text, which has the foreigners arriving in Bethlehem at the same time Mary and Joseph are there for registration and taxation. And, of course, we now know that Mary, Joseph, and Jesus are no doubt in a house, not a stable, from the very beginning. There is no need to have them move. The text matches the culture and chronology.

[102] (p 44) Since the biblical text does not specifically indicate where in the *East* the wise men are from, it is impossible to know how long it takes them to get to Jerusalem. If these foreigners are from the Fertile Crescent of the Tigris-Euphrates Valley of ancient Babylon, however, the trip would probably take them less than a month, traveling north and west around the Arabian Desert before heading south on The King's Highway.

In Genesis 31, Jacob secretly takes his wives, children, and flocks from Paddan-aram without informing Laban, his father-in-law. Three days after Jacob's escape, Laban finds out about Jacob's deception and takes off after Jacob. It takes Laban seven days in hot pursuit to catch up with Jacob, overtaking him in the hill country of Gilead opposite Palestine on the east side of the Jordan (Gen 31:17-23). Since northern Gilead is several days' journey from Jerusalem, and since the distance from the region of ancient Babylon to Paddan-aram is about the same as from Paddan-aram to Jerusalem, we conclude that it would have taken the wise men about three to four weeks to travel from ancient Babylon to Jerusalem.

If the wise men came from ancient Persia (further south and east of ancient Babylon), the trip would have taken longer. If they came from ancient Media (north of ancient Babylon) the trip could have been shorter.

The wise men undoubtedly travel south on The King's Highway, the main north-south trade route between the Fertile Crescent of Ancient Babylon in the north to the Gulf of Aqaba and beyond in the south. The wise men would have exited The Kings Highway and traveled west to the Jordan Valley, where they would have journeyed south to Jericho. The final leg of their journey would have taken them west, up through the Judean wilderness to Jerusalem. (See endnotes 45-46, p 78-80.)

[103] (p 44) Matthew 2:2.

[104] (p 46) Micah 5:2-6; Matthew 2:3-6. More than thirty years later, during Jesus' ministry in Jerusalem, the Jews rejected the possibility of Jesus being the Messiah since he was from Galilee: "*Others were saying, 'This is the Christ.' Still others were saying, 'Surely the Christ is not going to come from Galilee, is He? Has not the Scripture said that the Christ comes from the offspring of David, and from Bethlehem, the village where David was?'*" (Jn 7:41, 42). Apparently, no one checked out where Jesus had been born. The Jews assumed that since Jesus grew up in Galilee, He must have been born in Galilee.

The biblical text does not specifically say that King Herod informed the chief priests and scribes of the people why he wanted to know where the Christ was to be born. However, it seems reasonable to conclude that since the wise men were asking around Jerusalem as to where the King of the Jews had been born, between the word on the street and the question from King Herod, the chief priests and scribes had to know that these foreign astrologers believed the Messiah had been born.

Thirty-plus years later, however, there does not seem to be any historical awareness among the Jewish people or among the leaders of the Jews that a group of foreign astrologers had come to Jerusalem thirty years before declaring that the Messiah had been born, and that the chief priest and scribes of that day had said the Messiah was to be born in Bethlehem. Although King Herod was eager to check out the wise men's story for political reasons, the Jewish religious leaders apparently had no interest in further discussing or checking out the allegation for spiritual reasons.

[105] (p 46) Matthew 2:7-8.

[106] (p 46) Matthew 2:9-10. The biblical text does not say that the wise men follow the star from their homeland to Jerusalem. The traditional Christmas story assumes that they do. It is commonly held that the star disappears prior to the wise men's arrival in Jerusalem. Because they have no star to follow, the wise men are forced to stop in Jerusalem to ask for directions. This assumption probably stems from the fact that as

these foreigners leave Jerusalem for Bethlehem (per the information given them in Jerusalem), the strange star they had seen back home suddenly appears, uncharacteristically moves in front of them as they travel south, and then amazingly stops over the house where Mary, Joseph, and Jesus are staying.

It is very possible that the wise men (perhaps through divine revelation) link the kingly star with the Jewish expectations of a coming king and go to Jerusalem not because the star leads them there but because Jerusalem is the center of Judaism—the logical place for a Jewish king to be. They need no star to guide them on the first leg of their journey.

When the wise men leave Jerusalem, the star, which they have probably not seen now for quite some time, suddenly reappears, creating surprise and excitement. In fact, the wording of Matthew 2:9 suggests that when the star suddenly appears to the wise men as they head toward Bethlehem, this is the first they have seen the star since they saw it back home *in the east*. Matthew does not say, "*and the star that they had followed to Jerusalem went before them ....*" But rather, "*and lo, the star, which they had seen in the east, went on before them.*" (See endnote 96, pp 96-97.)

[107] (p 46) Matthew 2:9.

CHAPTER 14

[108] (p 48) On numerous occasions, the Old Testament refers to kings from the East bringing gifts to the kings (in some passages perhaps King [i.e., Messiah]) of Israel: "*The kings of Sheba and Seba offer gifts. And let all kings bow down before him. All nations serve him*" (Ps 72:10b, 11). "*All those from Sheba will come; they will bring gold and frankincense, and will bear good news of the praises of the LORD*" (Isa 60:6).

It should also be noted that although the gifts of frankincense and myrrh have been seen by some as symbolically foreshadowing Jesus' death (Nicodemus brought a large amount of myrrh and aloes for Jesus' burial, Jn 19:39), the wise men's three gifts might better symbolically foreshadow Jesus' high priestly ministry. In Exodus 30, the altar of incense (consistently associated with prayer in the Bible) was overlaid with <u>pure gold</u> (Ex 30:3) and upon that altar <u>frankincense</u> was burned perpetually (Ex 30:8). Additionally, the holy anointing oil (which we might call the "Scent of Holiness"), a uniquely blended perfume for anointing the tent of meeting, the ark of the testimony, all the furnishing of the tabernacle, as well as the high priest and his sons, was one-third <u>flowing myrrh</u> (500 parts flowing myrrh; 250 parts fragrant cinnamon; 250 parts fragrant cane; and 500 parts cassia, Ex 30:21-26). Anyone else smelling like that fragrance of holiness was to be cut off from his people (Ex 30:33). And finally, the perfume used only by the priests as their scent of holy distinction (which we might call "The Essence of God") consisted of four spices in equal parts—stacte, onycha, galbanum and <u>pure frankincense</u> (Ex 30:34). Anyone else wearing that scent would be cut off from his people (Ex 30:38).

While the above discussion is interesting and plausible, it is equally possible that the gifts have no special symbolic or spiritual significance at all. Selected simply because of their value and appropriateness for a king, the gifts may have been God's provision for Joseph and Mary, who would shortly be told by God to go *to* Egypt, just as God had gifts lavished upon the Children of Israel by the Egyptians when He commanded Israel to *leave* Egypt at the time of the Exodus (Ex 3:21-22; 12:35-36).

[109] (p 48) Matthew 2:11.

[110] (p 48) One can only speculate how long the foreigners stay and what it takes to provide food and lodging.

[111] (p 50) God's instruction to the wise men not to return home through Jerusalem poses a challenge to them since Jerusalem is the link to The King's Highway via the Jordan Valley. This leaves the wise men with two alternate route possibilities. Since Bethlehem does not have a road going due west out of town, one possibility is to head south toward Hebron. Some seven or eight mile south of Bethlehem, they come upon a

road going west, which takes them out of the hill country of Judah and down to the coastal plains of the Mediterranean Sea. The wise men then travel north on the trade route that runs along the coastal plain, cut through the Mountains of Carmel using the Megiddo Pass, travel down the Jezreel Valley where Nazareth is visible high on the northern ridge, go through Capernaum where Jesus later lives and ministers, then head northeast to link up with The King's Highway.

The other exit strategy is to head south and east through Tekoa, exiting the Judean Wilderness near Masada. Looping around the southern tip of the Dead Sea, they would proceed eastward until they hit The King's Highway.

The first option seems to me to be the shortest, and therefore the best, option. Either way, the wise men obey God.

CHAPTER 15

[112] (p 52) Matthew 2:13.

[113] (p 52) Matthew 2:14. The fact that Joseph and Mary have to leave during the night indicates a sense of urgency and immediacy. Perhaps that very night Herod makes the decision to kill all the boy babies in and around Bethlehem later that day.

[114] (p 52) Matthew 2:16-18. John (the Baptist) evidently lives far enough away from Bethlehem to be spared.

[115] (p 52) Hebron is located some 15 miles south of Bethlehem.

[116] (p 54) Matthew 2:1-3.

[117] (p 54) Matthew 2:4-6.

[118] (p 54) Matthew 2:3.

CHAPTER 16

[119] (p 55) Matthew 2:13. Delaying Joseph and family's return to Nazareth brought with it the additional advantage of putting Mary's pregnancy and the exact details and sequence of Joseph and Mary's relationship and pregnancy further and further into the past.

[120] (p 55) Matthew 2:15, 19-21. Hoehner demonstrates that Herod the Great dies sometime between March 29 and April 11, 4 B.C. (Hoehner 1977, 13). If Hoehner's conclusion is right that Jesus is born in late 5 B.C. (see endnote 40, p 68), then Mary and Joseph may have stayed in Egypt for no more than six months. (We do not know, however, how soon after Herod's death the angel of the Lord appears to Joseph in a dream.)

A.B. Bruce concludes that Herod the Great dies in Jericho about three years after Jesus' birth (Bruce 1967, 460). If Bruce is correct, Jesus would be two or three years old when Mary and Joseph return to Nazareth from Egypt.

It is easy to understand why Mary and Joseph need to flee Bethlehem to keep Baby Jesus from being killed in Herod's slaughter of infants in and around Bethlehem. Interestingly, while it is safe after Herod's death for Joseph and Mary and Jesus to return to Nazareth (Mt 2:20), traveling in the Jerusalem/Bethlehem region is considered dangerous. Since there is a near total absence of boys in a two-year age span, Jesus (being of that age span), could be conspicuous and raise all sorts of questions and/or memories which possibly could get back to Archelaus. The shepherds who visited Jesus the night he was born and all those who had gotten to know pregnant Mary before her child was born must have wondered about and discussed what had happened to Jesus. If Jesus would show up, that could cause quite a stir and again place Jesus in harm's way. We conclude this because when Joseph and family return to Nazareth after Herod the Great dies, the biblical text says, "*And he* [Joseph] *arose and took the Child and His mother, and come into the land of Israel. But when he heard that Archelaus was reigning over Judea in place of his father Herod, he was afraid to go there. And being warned by God in a dream, he departed for the regions of Galilee"* (Mt 2:21-22).

[121] (p 57) Matthew 2:22.
[122] (p 57) Matthew 2:23; Luke 2:29.

WORKS CITED

Bailey, Kenneth E. "The Manger and the Inn: The Cultural Background of Luke 2:7." *Evangelical Review of Theology* 4:2 (2003) : 201-217.

_____. "The Manger and the Inn." *Christian Leader* 66:12 (2003) : 4-7.

_____. "The Manger and the Inn." *Bible and Spade* 20:4 (2007) : 98-106.

Barclay, William. *The Gospel of Luke*. Philadelphia: The Westminster Press, 1975.

Bruce, A.B. "The Synoptic Gospels." In *The Expositor's Greek New Testament*, edited by W. Robertson Nicoll. Grand Rapids: Wm. B. Eerdmans Publishing Company, 1967.

Christie, C.M. Inn. James Orr, gen. ed. *The International Standard Bible Dictionary*. Vol. 3. Grand Rapids: Wm. B. Eerdmans Publishing Company, 1960.

Ferraro, Gary. *Cultural Anthropology: An Applied Perspective*. Belmont, California: Wadsworth/Thomson Learning, 2001.

Gower, Ralph. *The New Manners and Customs of Bible Times*. Chicago: Moody Press, 1987.

Harrison, Everett F. *Introduction to the New Testament*. Grand Rapids: Wm. B. Eerdmans Publishing Company, 1962.

Harrison, Everett F. and Charles F. Pfeiffer, eds. *The Wycliffe Bible Commentary*. Chicago: Moody Press, 1962.

Hoehner, Harold W. *Chronological Aspects of the Life of Christ*. Grand Rapids: Zondervan Publishing House, 1977.

Keener, Craig S. *Matthew*. Downers Grove, Illinois: InterVarsity Press, 1997.

Keil, C.F, and F Delitzsch. *Commentary on the Old Testament in Ten Volumes*. Vol. I. Grand Rapids, Michigan: William B. Eerdmans Publishing Company, 1973.

Laub, Karin. *New Look at Old Story*. Associated Press. December 10, 1994.

McHugh, John. *The Mother of Jesus in the New Testament*. Garden City, New York: Doubleday and Company, Inc, 1975.

Monson, Jim, gen. con. *Student Map Manual: Historical Geography of the Bible Lands*. Jerusalem: Pictorial Archive (Near Eastern History) Est. and Survey of Israel, 1979.

Murphy-O'Conner, Jerome. *The Holy Land*. New York: Oxford University Press, 1998.

Pax, Wolfgang E. *In the Footsteps of Jesus*. Jerusalem: Nateev and Steimatzky Publishing, 1973.

Smalley, Gary and John Trent. *The Blessing*. New York: Thomas Nelson Publishers, 1986.

Thomson, William. *The Land and the Book*, Vol. II. New York: Harper and Brothers, 1858, 1871.

Vine, W.E., Merrill Unger and William White, Jr., *Vine's Complete Expository Dictionary of Old and New Testament Words*. Nashville: Thomas Nelson Publishing, 1996.

Wheat, Ed and Gaye Wheat. *Intended for Pleasure: Sex Technique and Sexual Fulfillment in Christian Marriage*. Old Tappan, New Jersey: Fleming H. Revell Company, 1977.

Wilkins, Michael J. *The NIV Application Commentary: Matthew*. Grand Rapids: Zondervan Publishing House, 2004.